Whether you are pro-life or p
powerful story by Jacqueline
trauma of abortion, she lived with guilt for many years until she
found forgiveness and hope in the gospel of Jesus Christ. Now
she's an advocate for both unborn children and the women who
bear them. This book will break your heart in all the right ways
and give you sympathy for the difficult decisions so many women
face alone. Read this book and share it with others, and then roll
up your sleeves and fight for the dignity of mothers and children.

—Daniel Darling, VP of communications, Ethics and Religious
Liberty Commission
Author of several books, including *The Dignity Revolution*

WHITE STICK

WHITE STICK

REDEMPTION
PRESS

Jaqueline Middler

Published by Redemption Press, PO Box 427, Enumclaw, WA 98022.

Toll-Free (844) 2REDEEM (273-3336)

Redemption Press is honored to present this title in partnership with the author. The views expressed or implied in this work are those of the author. Redemption Press provides our imprint seal representing design excellence, creative content, and high-quality production.

The author has tried to recreate events, locales, and conversations from her memories of them. In order to maintain their anonymity, in some instances she has changed the names of individuals and may have changed some identifying characteristics and details, such as physical properties, occupations, and places of residence.

Unless otherwise indicated, all Scripture quotations are taken from the Holy Bible, New International Version, copyright ©1973, 1978, 1984, 2011 by Biblica, Inc.® Used by permission. All rights reserved worldwide.

ISBN: 978-1-68314-921-7 (Paperback)

Library of Congress Catalog Card Number: 2019919903

I dedicate this book to my Lord and King, the one and only God Almighty, who rescued me from the depths of despair, and to his Son, Jesus, who sacrificed so much so I would be able to have communion with him. My life, my mission, and my purpose are dedicated to him. I can't wait to serve in the kingdom of heaven, and I hope to see you there.

Contents

Acknowledgments

As with any major undertaking, it takes a village. When I told God that I would be his voice at that concert all those years ago, I did not realize what it was I would do and who would help me along the way. I would like to first thank God and his plan. He has come through for me more times then I even remember, and his continued love and grace gives me confidence to pursue his dreams for me.

I would be lost without my husband and our lovely children, and I thank them for allowing me to spend time away from them to write this book.

Thank you to my parents, who were willing to relive this time with me and give me honest feedback and support.

To my best friends (my girls), the women who have heard my story and loved me anyways, who invest in my life and our friendship—you bring joy to my life.

Thank you to the people who first read that 9,000-word manuscript and gave me feedback.

Thank you to my friends back home and the encouragement they have given me.

Thank you to Michelle for being willing to talk with me repeatedly about how to rewrite this book and helping me to find the right voice.

Thank you to Dan Darling and his wife, Angela, for taking a vested interest in my book and helping me navigate through self-publishing and marketing.

This book would not have gotten off the ground without a good editor, and I had one of the best—thank you Sue Fairchild for all the emails and back and forth, for understanding my heart and being willing to listen.

Without the expert advice and quality product, this book would have never gotten to you, the reader, and so I have to thank Athena and her expert crew at Redemption Press for making exceptions for me and holding my hand through this process—I am excited to see how God continues to bless you.

I also want to thank the men and women who have been fighting for the rights of the unborn and their mothers, and thank you to the countless thousands who give of their time and money for these precious souls.

I finally I want to thank you, the reader, who is willing to go on this journey with me through one of the darkest periods of my life—thank you and God bless!

Introduction

For you created my inmost being;
you knit me together in my mother's womb.
I praise you because I am fearfully
and wonderfully made;
Psalm 139:13–14

*W*hen I was a college student, I chose to terminate two of my pregnancies. I justified each by accepting rationalizations that are often provided to pregnant women. At the time, I felt I had done the right thing. I could simply "move on" from these moments and create the life I'd always dreamed of living. What I didn't know then was that I wouldn't move on. I would continue to struggle internally with the effects of these decisions for years.

In recent years my family and I have acknowledged my abortions, but I have been unwilling to dive deeply into the topic for fear of hurting them more than I already have. One of my deepest regrets is choosing to tell them what I'd done. I could have kept them in the dark as I did many others. However, had I not told my family then, I might not be telling my story now. I most likely would have hidden these experiences deep inside my heart, locked away forever.

Even though I'd kept that shame and deep pain locked away, it became a persistent part of my life. I turned to drugs and alcohol to numb the pain. But those superficial things didn't erase the guilt I felt inside. The effects of choosing abortion lingered in my life, and subsequently, I made other poor choices as a result.

One day I opened my NIV Bible to Genesis and read the story of creation. I had heard this story many times, but I had never read it for myself. Suddenly, the words came alive. I know now that God opened my heart to him in that moment. I began to seek him. As I read more, he opened my heart further. God pursued me. He spoke his words to me, and they resonated. He opened my broken heart and fractured soul and poured his living water into them.

Even after I became a Christian, those years of pain and guilt were not automatically erased. However, I started to learn more about myself and my choices. I was a murderer. I had sinned. I found it hard to forgive myself and didn't know how God or anyone else could either. As I began to walk with God and read his Word, I tried to see myself as he sees me. I also began to talk with women who shared their abortion stories with me. Many felt the same shame, guilt, and pain that I had felt since my abortions. The reality of these women's stories and how they related to mine helped ease some of my pain, but I wondered how women could overcome the effects of choosing abortion. How could women like me know they were not alone?

As I continued to seek God's promises, I felt a nudging to be a voice for these kinds of women. Their story is mine—one of heartache—but also redemption. I want women to understand how choosing abortion has lasting effects on your heart, mind, and soul. I want to share my story, my personal journey toward redemption, to help others who have also made these choices. I long to share the hope I now have.

This book is an honest and vivid look at how one decision to abort a baby can forever change your soul. Within these pages, I offer an eyewitness account of the abortion experience. It is raw and straightforward and, perhaps, hard for some to understand. But my story also speaks to the heart of God's undying love and grace and how his mercy brings forgiveness. My story is about the lasting effects of shame and guilt, but also about the power of God's Word to heal.

I'm not trying to change laws, but only to give an honest look at how one individual can be affected by choosing abortion. For me, taking the life of an unborn child left scars, vast holes within that could only be filled with the one true God.

This is my story, but it is also the story of many other women. I pray it will shine a light into the dark places we hide.

Chapter 1

Saying Yes

"For I know the plans I have for you," declares the Lord,
"plans to prosper you and not to harm you, plans to give
you hope and a future."
Jeremiah 29:11

I looked down at the skinny white stick dripping with my urine and watched as the liquid spread to the two tiny ovals. Immediately, a line formed in the first box. I clenched my eyes and prayed that the other line would not appear. Less than a second later, the other line appeared and confirmed my worst fears. I still tried to will the line away, the second line that would transform my life. However, no amount of willpower could change the fact. I was pregnant.

My eyes started to swim with unshed tears. I threw the stick on the counter and grabbed the box, attempting to read the directions through the blur. Maybe two lines meant I *wasn't* carrying a little life inside me. After repeatedly looking from the directions to the stick and back again, the truth hit me. I gasped. This couldn't be happening to me.

I was a nineteen-year-old freshman in college, looking at a little white stick that could change my entire life in three short minutes.

My dormmates pounded on the door to the bathroom, asking for my response, but I sat mute. I looked in the mirror and suddenly didn't recognize the person standing in front of me. Was this the same girl who'd said she'd wait until she married to have sex? My innocence gone, I found myself facing a responsibility I wasn't ready for. How had I not even thought to use protection? My family were strict Catholics and went to church every Sunday, and my parents had taught me right from wrong. I had even argued against providing condoms in high school because doing so would lead to premarital sex. Where had I gone wrong? I searched my mind through the last six months and tried to find the point at which I'd lost my direction.

My family was military and we moved a lot, but my childhood had been a good one. In fact, I thought the constant moving had created an adventurous spirit in me—we were always experiencing new things. Perhaps that adventurous spirit, which I'd always admired within myself, had led me here.

I thought back to the summer between my freshman and sophomore years of high school. We'd moved to a small town, and I'd left many friends behind. I had just turned sixteen and started working my first real job in a fish cannery in our new town. The job allowed me to make extra money and meet new people. Even though the smell was awful and stuck to my skin for days, the work was fun. I enjoyed working on a team and meeting new people—who were mostly college kids who had come to Alaska for the summer. I became the foreman's favorite and got pulled off the line to work special jobs, although putting my arm down a drain to clear out week-old salmon guts doesn't seem so special now.

I loved being liked by others—I enjoyed the attention. I didn't realize then how much of myself I would be willing to sacrifice to feel needed, wanted, and chosen.

From that summer on, I thrived on working hard. I started my eighth new school that August and had to navigate through all the pitfalls of being the new girl. Right away, a boy started paying attention to me, and I was naïve enough to think he really liked me. One of the girls in my class told me to stay away from him, but I didn't listen. However, it quickly became apparent I was not the only one he was hanging out with, and he soon ended up leaving me for another girl. Thankfully, I was still innocent in the art of sexual relations, and I hadn't gone far with him. I continued to adjust and made a few friends. I started playing basketball and joined the band and dance team. However, fitting in is not the same as belonging.

Then the shop teacher, whom I didn't know, asked if I wanted to join a vocational club. At first I declined, thinking it was not my thing. Then he told me I'd be able to go to the state conference in my old town. And I could stay for a week. I missed my friends and longed to see them. This would be the perfect opportunity to do just that. "Sign me up," I said.

The next week I met with the shop teacher, and he explained how the club worked. I would have to compete in one of the many vocational competitions. I chose cooking. I loved to cook whole dinners for my family and friends and would spend many hours planning the appetizer, salads, soups, main course, sides, and dessert. I enjoyed cooking for hours and setting the table with dishes for each course. My mom encouraged my love of cooking, even though I'm sure I was not as adept at the cleanup.

One of the items judged as part of the cooking competition was creativity. I spent many hours looking through my cookbooks for something unique, eventually choosing a bunny salad. The salad used pears for the body, raisins for the eyes, and a dab of cottage cheese for the tail. With minimum ingredients, the salad was easy and fun to make.

Before the state competition, it was mandatory to attend the club's monthly meeting. During one of those meetings, my teacher asked me if I was interested in signing up for a state officer position. I laughed and declined. I hated speaking in front of a crowd. Just the thought of speaking gave me butterflies in my stomach. Honestly, I wanted to do the bare minimum for this club just to see my old friends. However, my teacher saw something special in me—something I didn't see.

Before I knew it, we were on our way to the state conference. Because we'd been delayed by weather, the conference had already started when we arrived. We left our luggage with the front desk agent and were directed to one of the main ballrooms. I was shocked by the number of people. Our little group only had ten people, but hundreds crowded the ballroom. We tried to find open seats and not interrupt the speaker. We found seats in the far back corner and settled in.

I tried to focus on the meeting, but everything sounded foreign to me. It seemed like they were accepting nominations for the different state offices. My ears perked up as I heard them call for nominees for the office of reporter because this was the office my teacher had asked me about. Five kids made their way to the front. I was relieved I had said no. There was no way I wanted to stand up in front of everyone and talk about something I knew nothing about.

Then I heard my name. The shock on my face must have been apparent as I looked around the room, thinking they had made a mistake. The room had grown silent, and everyone was looking around to find me. Time stopped. My eyes darted to my teacher as I heard the speaker say, "Will Jacqueline Gerhauser please stand up." I started to shake my head and felt my eyes bugging out as my heart rate increased. Then my teacher nudged me on my back and told me to stand up. I stood on shaky legs while not breaking eye contact with my teacher, who was smiling up at me.

The speaker asked, "Do you accept the nomination for state reporter?"

My eyes darted toward the speaker.

"Say yes," my teacher said. "You have to say yes!"

"No," I whispered. But when I looked around, hundreds of eyes gawked back at me. A quiet hush had settled over the crowd as everyone waited to hear what I would say. I fought the urge to run, took a deep breath, and said, "Yes."

The speaker motioned for me to come to the front. Before doing so, I turned to my teacher and said, "I'm going to kill you!" He just smiled and laughed. Before I knew it, I was being whisked away to give an introductory speech in front of all those people—with no clue what to say.

Looking back now, I know that was a life-defining, life-changing moment. That day opened my life to all the other yes decisions I would make—most of them simply to please others. Being part of that group trained me in leadership as well as in organizational and life skills. It also gave me the courage to say yes to many other things. Yes, I would try any sport, even if I was bad at it. Yes, I would go on that trip. Yes, I would take that jump. Yes, I would try, even if I failed. I said yes to many wonderful things and achieved many.

The first set of yeses in my life set me on a course to excel. I made the jazz band. I played with the team. I got straight As. I had friends, went on adventures, saw the world, led an organization, and got a full-tuition waiver to college. Saying yes to those things built my future and set me apart.

However, the word "yes" also led me down a destructive path. Yes, I will have unprotected sex. Yes, I will drink that beer. Yes, I will smoke marijuana. Yes, I will give in to fear and shame.

Saying yes to those things brought me to my current situation—sitting in my dorm-room bathroom wondering what I'd do next.

I looked in the mirror again, held that little white stick, took a deep breath, and said, "Yes. Yes, I am pregnant." I turned and opened the door. The look of shock and disbelief on my friends' faces mirrored my own. My voice broke, and my eyes filled with tears. "What am I going to do?" I hoped someone would tell me. This felt like a dream. This could not be happening to me. I needed to call my boyfriend.

I barely remember dialing his number. The phone rang and rang. Eventually someone answered, and then my boyfriend came to the phone. After taking a deep breath, I told him the news.

"Are you serious?" he asked.

"Yes. Please come back. I need you."

"No, I can't. I want to stay and visit my friends. I can't come back until Monday."

Shock, outrage, and despair poured through my body. This was the worst thing that had happened in my life, and he wouldn't return to me? I needed him, needed someone. He had just as much to do with this as I did, and yet he didn't seem fazed at all. As I hung up the phone, I felt more alone than I ever had.

Our relationship had already been showing strain. As with many young loves, we had an emotional and physical connection but little mutual respect. We didn't put each other first, but thought only of our own feelings and needs. We rarely thought about the friendship, the loyalty, and the selflessness we would need to have a long-term relationship. Now I was pregnant, and he—only the second boy I'd ever slept with—didn't seem to care.

I had focused on scholarships, not boyfriends, in high school. However, in the spring of my senior year I became involved with a boy who had stolen my heart. We had a quick connection and a fast friendship. One night we dove further into exploring each other and went too far. As he pushed forward, I let go and allowed it to happen. We hadn't planned to have sex, and there was nothing romantic about the moment. It was nothing like I thought my first time would be. Afterward I cried—disappointed that I had broken my promise to God and myself to wait. I had been a willing participant, but not an active leader. I allowed sex to happen to me. I didn't take control or think about the consequences. I was young and naïve. I was in love and it had felt good. But we both knew sex before marriage was wrong and quickly promised each other we'd never do it again. And we never did.

By the time I started college, I had experienced a lot of other firsts: the first time I smoked marijuana, the first time I got drunk, the first time I left my family and lived alone, the first time I felt free, the first time I made all my own decisions, and the first time I suffered the consequences of those decisions. These firsts defined most of my adult life. It's easy to say yes to something that makes you feel good or happy in the moment, but sometimes saying yes has lasting consequences.

My first term at college, I continued the pattern of trying to fit in. I went to parties, but drank water, thinking I could keep a clearer head that way. Soon everyone wanted me to drink and party with them. I was offered alcohol and drugs more times than I could count. However, I kept my promise to myself and the boy back home and didn't give in to those temptations. My roommates took me under their wings, making the transition easier. That first term, I experienced more firsts. I had my eyebrows plucked, bought a pair of Calvin Klein jeans—which replaced my normal long skirts—and started wearing makeup full time. My friends back home wouldn't recognize this new me, but I loved her. I had a chameleon's heart and changed myself to fit in with wherever I was and whomever I was with. I hadn't yet discovered the real me.

I enjoyed that first term—enjoyed the freedom I felt. At times I couldn't believe I'd left my rural, rustic home in Alaska for the big city life. When I looked at those towering concrete mountains and the steady stream of cars, I wondered how I'd ended up here. But every new experience fed into my adventuresome spirit. I loved all of it and was doing well in my classes. I was happy, but a tad homesick.

In November, just before my first term ended, I met a boy. He seemed different from anyone I had ever met. Adventurous and exciting, he was the life of any party and was willing to try new things. His dreadlocks and crystal-blue eyes made him seem wild to me. I felt free and beautiful with him. I loved his carefree spirit, and he made me laugh.

Before I knew it, we were a couple. My new boyfriend invited me to my first concert, and we partied afterward. The night was wild, and I don't remember much except I had fun. The exciting lifestyle he lived was unlike anything I was used to, and it drew me like a moth to a flame. I never thought about getting burned.

We spoke a lot about sex, but I told him time and again I wouldn't do it. I was naïve enough to think we could progressively make out but avoid the act of sex. However, once you open one door, it's hard to shut it, but very easy to kick it wide open and walk through. I started allowing life to simply happen to me without making active choices or thinking things completely through. I lived only in the moment.

I cried after our first time, knowing my innocence had been sacrificed again. As I looked again at that white stick now, I wished I had taken a moment to consider these consequences.

Once we'd had sex that first time, it was hard for me to say no, and I continued to have sex with him without protection. It wasn't that I didn't know about birth control. I wasn't stupid. I simply didn't consider the consequences of not using protection. I was not prepared to have safe sex because, in my mind, I wasn't supposed to be having sex in the first place. I rode on the edge of the cliff. I enjoyed the view but never thought I would fall. How wrong I was! You can't walk near the edge without slipping.

My boyfriend's wild spirit led us to have sex in odd places and even in front of others. Shame and guilt quickly replaced my innocence, but somehow I was not willing to speak up to stop it. He never forced me—I was simply afraid I would lose him, so I kept accepting. I tried hard to make our relationship work because in some corner of my mind I thought staying with him would reconcile the pieces of myself I had given away.

Unfortunately, not only did it *not* help with the broken bits of myself, but the crazy parties and odd sexual encounters further added to my guilt and shame. I began silencing that shame and guilt by using drugs—mostly marijuana. One quick puff would quiet my internal thoughts. When I was high, life was good. When I started to feel the shame and guilt creeping back in, I got high.

Now, as I listened to the click of the phone and turned toward my two roommates, I realized how wrong I had been to try to make our relationship work. Even though I'd worked hard to make him happy, he wasn't supporting me. I was on my own. I grabbed the phone and called my parents. As the phone rang in my ear, more regrets filled my mind. Instead of the typical college student phone call to talk about grades or to request money and food, I was calling to deliver horrible news. I felt the tears of desperation stream down my face as my mom answered. Without thinking, I blurted out, "I'm pregnant."

My declaration was met with silence. I tried to fill that silence with more words as I sought to offer an explanation, but no words could lessen the shock. In hindsight, telling my parents this news only added to my list of regrets. This wasn't how we'd planned my college life or future. Instead of finishing my first year of college with good grades and making my parents proud, I now carried their first grandchild.

During the phone call, Mom asked if I was sure, and then she asked what I was going to do. I had no idea. I wanted someone to tell me what to do. I didn't want this to be happening. I wanted to go back to yesterday . . . or before I'd ever had sex. In the end, I told her I would think about my choices and call her back.

After our conversation, I lay on my bed, tears falling in disbelief. I knew plenty of girls who were having sex and hadn't gotten pregnant. Why me? My mind spun in a thousand circles. Maybe the test was wrong. Maybe I would have a miscarriage. I envisioned myself with a baby and then imagined the whispers and shame I'd endure. I envisioned my dreams flushed down the toilet as I held a screaming baby on my hip. How had I screwed up my life so badly?

I rehashed my despair to my roommates that weekend until I hated the sound of my voice. My parents called me a couple of times, but we only spoke about my options. One: have the baby. Two: give up the baby. Three: have an abortion. Throughout most of my life my parents usually had an opinion and happily directed me in what to do, whether I wanted them to or not. I wanted them to decide for me now as they had done in the past. However, now they remained mostly silent as they listened to my endless chattering. The choice was mine, they said. In my mind, I had no choice.

The minutes of the weekend clicked by slowly as I waited for my boyfriend to return. When he finally arrived, we stared at each other in disbelief. Then he reached out to me and I hugged him. After clinging to each other for several moments, we discussed our options.

Chapter 2

Choices

*If anyone, then, knows the good they ought to do and
doesn't do it, it is sin for them.*
James 4:17

*I*t's funny how life moves forward and people go about their
lives, even when yours is falling apart. My boyfriend and I held
each other through the night as we cried and talked about our options while my roommates withdrew and allowed us space. They
continued moving forward in their lives.

Tuesday morning I woke with a start. My boyfriend had left
sometime in the early morning for his classes. My roommates now
also prepared for classes, but I simply sat on my bed too shell-
shocked to move. I could not reconcile my normal life with this
new life growing inside me. When my roommates left with a click
of the lock, I was alone. I had to go to class, but the weight bearing
down on me kept me still, paralyzed. Then I felt a wave of nausea.
I hadn't eaten much over the weekend due to my emotional stress,
but now I felt as if I would vomit. I barely made it to the bathroom.
Afterward, I decided I needed to face the day, so I took a shower.

In one of our last phone conversations, my mother had suggested I go to the clinic on campus for a medical opinion. On the way to my first class, I again felt the urge to vomit and barely made it to the garbage can outside the classroom.

The morning sickness proved the test hadn't been wrong. I couldn't deny my situation. My mind could not comprehend how just four short days ago I had been worried about what I would do for the weekend, and now I was vomiting in random trash cans in the hallway. I felt as if my baby was punishing me for my choices. How had my body betrayed me this much?

After my last class, I walked to the clinic and told the nurse my worst fear—I thought I was pregnant. She gave me a ton of different brochures and pamphlets spelling out all my options. Some showed smiling people holding a baby. Some showed little feet and arms. They all included a lot of numbers to call. With all the brochures in hand, I asked the nurse, "What should I do?"

She gave me a hug and told me I would find my way. "The choice is yours."

Her words did not comfort me any more than my parents' had. I didn't want to make this choice. I didn't want to "find my way." I wanted someone to tell me what to do.

After leaving the clinic, I walked aimlessly for a while and ended up on a bench in a park. The empty park matched the emptiness I felt inside. Now that my morning sickness had subsided a bit, it seemed easy to forget about the child in my belly. I started to read through all the pamphlets, but had to stop numerous times to wipe my tears away. I didn't want to read about these options. I simply didn't want to be pregnant. I could feel myself disconnecting from the life growing inside me.

The words continued to blur as I read about horrific abortion procedures, who to call if I wanted an abortion, how many people longed for a baby but could not have one, and the plethora of help I could receive if I chose to keep the baby.

I quickly decided I couldn't give my child away. That choice felt worse than any other for some reason. I thought about all the unwanted kids in our foster-care system who wondered every day why their parents had given them up. In the end, my choice not to give away my baby was based solely on fear and needing control. I wanted to have a say in what happened to my baby. I knew I would not be able to give my baby up once he or she were born.

I know now from many friends who have adopted that adoption, while difficult for the birth mother, is a great decision for the baby. Many couples want to have a baby, but for various reasons cannot. A birth mother's willingness to give up her baby allows someone else to love an otherwise unwanted baby. However, it's hard to go through nine months of pregnancy knowing you will still end up alone. Although I can't imagine that choice even today, I wonder if my soul would have been less fractured had I made this choice.

In that moment, sitting on that park bench, I did not want to keep this baby. I wanted this entire situation simply to be over. However, I didn't think I could kill my baby either. I just wanted the whole situation to go away. Disappear. Fade into obscurity. My choices demanded consequences, but instead of accepting them, I hid from them, hoping they'd go away.

I walked the long way back to my dorm room, where I found my boyfriend waiting for me. I showed him all the options in the brochures, and we again talked about our choices. I leaned toward continuing the pregnancy, but hoped for a miscarriage. We talked about the possibility and dreamed a little about what it would be like to have the baby. We laughed, and he held my stomach. Even though I felt the only moral option was to have the baby, I felt no joy with that decision, only desperation. I hung on to the hope that my pregnancy would not be healthy and I would miscarry. I even told my roommates and my parents I had decided to keep the baby. Although I was extremely scared and unhappy and hoped the life inside me would die, I still clung to my belief system that killing a baby was wrong.

I realize now how lost and far away from God I must have been at that time—despite thinking I was doing the right thing. How scared and alone I must have felt to hope that the life growing inside me would die. In the last year, I had distanced myself from God. I had focused on the energies of the universe—not on the Creator of the universe. I had adopted a concept of energy and connection, but never thought to reach out to the God who created us. Perhaps I felt numb from that first bad decision—separated from God by my shame. I let the darkness of my sin rule, and God's light seemed dim. I know now that if I had reached for God, he would have come through with an army of light. But I was too lost in my own sin.

Shortly after my boyfriend left, the telephone rang. It was a friend, who had helped me adjust to college life, returning my call to her. I had reached out to get her thoughts. I felt desperate for someone to tell me what to do. She was a couple of years older than I was and had taken me under her wing. After hearing of my situation, she said she would help. I held on to that phone like a lifeline and readily agreed to meet her.

The next afternoon I met with my friend and told her I planned to keep the baby but hoped for a miscarriage. I held on to this hope like a drowning person holding on to a life raft. My friend looked me in the eyes and said, "You're healthy and young. It's almost 100 percent certain that you will have a healthy pregnancy and baby."

Her words ripped through my plan, making me realize I hoped for an outcome I didn't want to choose.

She began talking to me about how amazing I was, how much I still had to do with my life, and how this baby would change all of that. She reminded me of my scholarship and about how I wouldn't be able to live out the dream my boyfriend and I had created where we live together, finish school, and live happily ever after. That dream simply wasn't feasible now. She laid out how hard it would be to have and care for a baby. In the end, she stripped me of my naïvety and forced me to face the reality of the situation.

That reality hit me hard. I couldn't breathe. When my friend noticed the beginning of a panic attack, she shared with me what had happened to her. She had gotten pregnant with her boyfriend the year before and had chosen abortion. She was open and honest with me about her experience. She never said it was easy, and she even shared that she had cried for many months after her abortion. Then she said, "But look at me now! I'm happy, and life has moved on."

Even though she and her boyfriend had broken up afterward, she did look happy. She was living the life I so desperately wanted.

"But I can't kill my baby," I said. After all, I had a hard time killing bugs and had even once rescued an ant that had a broken leg. Ever since I was a little girl, I'd had a soft heart. I always felt bad for the animals my dad hunted and killed. I remember one time he brought home a cooler full of ducks, and we had to pluck them. I looked into their lifeless eyes and felt sad. My parents would find me talking to the salmon Dad caught as they lay gasping for breath. My brothers made fun of me and my dad shook his head, but at that time I really valued life and felt bad when people or animals were hurting.

"It's only a group of cells now. It doesn't feel anything," my friend said. "It's not even a formed baby at all. This is the perfect time to end your pregnancy—before it becomes an actual baby."

Finally, words that comforted me. I wouldn't be killing a baby—just a group of cells. I held on to those words.

If I chose to keep the baby, I'd have to give up my scholarship and live with my parents—things I had worked so hard to accomplish and get away from. To go back home in failure and disgrace felt like more than I could handle. I continued listening to my friend and silenced the nagging doubt building up inside. If I chose to abort my baby, I could pretend this had never happened to me. No one would know unless I told them. It would be like it never happened—exactly what I wanted.

I realize now that although my friend looked happy, sometimes the deepest scars lie in places you can't see. Finding a person who will say the things you want to hear may seem like you've found your savior and can be easier than listening for the true Savior's voice.

My friend gave me the number for Planned Parenthood. When I returned to my dorm room, my boyfriend was waiting for me once more. We huddled inside the bathroom—the only place that had a door and privacy—and I told him I had decided to get an abortion. He sat on the toilet and looked up at me with sad eyes. "Why?"

I looked into his blue eyes and saw a mixture of relief and anguish that mirrored my own. He put his arms around me and we started to cry. I cried because this was happening to me. I cried because I had lost myself. I cried because I had to make this decision. I cried because I knew—deep down—that this decision was wrong. But I saw no other way out.

My boyfriend held me tight. "I keep thinking about those little feet on that one pamphlet," he said into my hair.

I felt myself stiffen. I pulled back. I had to harden my heart to follow this plan. I had to pretend this had never happened. I couldn't think about those tiny feet or dreams of a family. This was the beginning of the break in our relationship and my soul.

The next morning, I called my parents and told them I was going to have an abortion. Again, my statement was met with silence. I wanted them to yell and tell me how horrible I was to kill their first grandchild. I wanted them to tell me not to do it. I always wanted to please them, and I knew this decision disappointed and hurt them, but I still wanted them to tell me no, that they wouldn't allow it. I wanted them to rage at me, to list all the reasons why I could not do this. I needed to hear it.

Instead, my mom said, "We do not agree or support this choice, but it is your choice to make."

I felt alone, but I had already hardened my heart and knew, somehow, that abortion would be the easiest solution for everyone involved. Once I made the decision, I never wavered. I became like a solider going to battle, determined to win and get my life back on track. Little did I know that I had already lost the war.

Most of that first week of pregnancy went by in a blur. As soon as I made the decision to terminate my baby, my body seemed to rebel, and I started vomiting even more. I felt so tired and sick physically and emotionally. I forced myself to focus on the plan and not retching. I still went to my classes and still talked and laughed, but on the inside I felt numb. As I prepared to terminate this life, I began to shut down.

I don't remember or clearly recall much of that week, but one thing I do remember is feeling lost. I felt as if I were lost at sea with no boat, waves crashing against me. I did not think about God or my faith during this time. Perhaps, subconsciously, I thought God had abandoned me as I had abandoned him.

My friend faithfully checked in with me and told me everything would be okay. She reassured me I was making the right choice and that everything would work out. She reminded me that the mass in my body was not a baby yet, but only cells.

But I know better now. At this point, my baby would have had a heartbeat. He or she would have already been forming little hands and toes. He or she would have been more than just cells.

I know the choice was mine though—not hers. I hold no blame in my heart for my friend. She had been willing to provide help and companionship, to attempt to guide me the only way she knew how. I only wished she would have known how that choice would fracture my soul. I wish she could have seen into the future and the many years after this when I would close my eyes and see visions of bloody baby parts and wonder if I had made the right choice.

When my friend called me the following week, I told her the date and time of my appointment. She agreed to drive me and one of my roommates. Even though it had only been ten days since I had found out I was pregnant, it felt like a lifetime had passed. I longed for the carefree days I'd enjoyed before knowing. I longed for freedom from my emotional turmoil.

Had I known then what I know now, my roommate and I would never have stepped into my friend's car on that fateful day. The emotional torment I sought so desperately to escape would follow me for many years. I would make many more choices that would fracture my soul into so many pieces that only the loving hands of my Savior could piece them back together. At nineteen—just beginning my adult life—I was on my way to making the worst decision I could ever make simply because I was afraid of ruining my life and of what others would think of me.

Those feelings haunted me for decades. Even now they creep into my thoughts and actions. It is only through trusting God's plan for me—knowing I matter to him and that I am not bound by every bad decision I have made or will make—that I have found freedom.

My boyfriend could not bring himself to come. He felt broken by what I was about to do. I know he didn't want the responsibility of a baby, but he knew these cells were alive. He knew I was going to end a life.

The drive to the abortion clinic seemed long and short at the same time. Every time we stopped, I wondered if I should jump out and run away. As my hand gripped the door, I hardened my heart and talked myself into the decision I had already agreed to. This baby wasn't a baby—only cells—and this was the best choice for my life. I could pretend this hadn't happened and move on with my life. Everything would go back to normal. I would have my life back.

Chapter 3

Reality of My Choice

For you created my inmost being; you knit me together in my mother's womb. I praise you because I am fearfully and wonderfully made.
Psalm 139:13–14

My eyes widened as we turned down the street to the abortion clinic. In front of the clinic, a crowd had formed and was blocking the entrance. I was unprepared for all the people who would be protesting my decision. My friend put a hand on my shoulder and told me not to look as we pulled in. I turned my head away. I had seen those signs and posters as I had driven by other clinics. I didn't want to see them today. I wanted to live in the fairy tale I had created in my mind.

My friend turned off the engine, and I realized the music in her car had covered the sounds of the protestors' screams. I couldn't make out what they were saying, yet the noise made me uneasy. As I began to doubt my decision, I heard a tap on my window and looked up to see the sweet, smiling face of a woman I had never met. She motioned for me to get out of the car.

I opened the door and the noises crescendoed. I hesitated for a moment, and the woman took my arm. "Come on, let's go."

I looked around and saw the faces of the men and women yelling at me. Their voices pleaded with me.

"Don't do this."

"God wouldn't want you to do this."

"We will help you. We will take care of your baby. Please, come, let us help you."

Their words confused me. How could they help me? What were they going to do? I didn't want to be pregnant. I didn't want to give this baby away. I wanted to pretend it never happened. Who were these people, and how did they know it would work out better if I had this baby?

In any battle, once it looks like defeat is near, the fight intensifies. In this battle, the same proved true. The lines in this battle have been clearly drawn by our laws and the media creating misleading perceptions. On one side are "close-minded" people who want to control your life and make you fear judgment. On the other side, "open-minded" people are willing to kill babies to allow women the freedom of choice. People on both sides are choosing what they think is right. But we have a history of situations that prove that just because someone thinks a choice is right does not mean it is. When people supported slavery, they thought it was right. When people supported Hitler, they thought it was right. When we look back on these events, we realize the errors of these choices.

Looking back on this day, I knew abortion was wrong. There is no real freedom, no real happiness, when you choose abortion. The "freedom" I chose became a prison sentence for my soul. Are there medical reasons for some pregnancies to end? Yes. However, laws that give women carte blanche to terminate any baby is not freedom for all.

I am writing this book to help both sides understand what thoughts went on inside my nineteen-year-old mind. The lines did not seem to be black and white, but gray.

As I neared the entrance, the protestors' voices changed. Compassionate pleading turned to indignant anger. Helpful consolation turned to condemnation. "We'll help you" turned to "How dare you, you murderer! God will judge you!"

I remember feeling shocked, then angry. Who did these people think they were? Had they spent the last ten days crying and agonizing over this decision? They didn't know me. As their hate-filled voices continued to scream at me, I became more determined to have the abortion. They couldn't scare me into a different decision. Their anger simply hardened my heart. In the minute it took to move from the car to the front door, my already frayed nerves became even more rattled. When the woman who held my arm pulled me into the clinic, I willingly went.

In the defining moments of your life you can close your eyes and remember specific sights, sounds, and smells. It's almost as if your brain takes a snapshot or short video of that moment so you can revisit it later. When the experience is beautiful, those snapshots are wonderful. The snapshots of this moment only tormented me in the years ahead.

The first thing I noticed upon entering the clinic was the silence. The yelling and screaming faded away. I realized the building must have had soundproof windows. The quiet gave me an immediate sense of calm, and I almost forgot why I was there.

The reception desk sat in an empty waiting room. A fish tank and walls painted in warm shades of blue and yellow lent a peaceful aura to the space. Everything felt calm about this place. The receptionist took my name, and then I sat down next to my friend and roommate and waited to be called. I did not sit long. My roommate smiled at me as I stood, and she said, "You can do this."

I felt like a lamb being led to slaughter, but the slaughter was not my own.

Inside another warm and inviting room, a quiet, gentle nurse asked me all kinds of questions and checked my vital signs. When she asked if I wanted anesthesia, I declined. Although I'd convinced myself the baby was only a group of cells and not a baby, some part of me knew that what I was doing was wrong, and I wanted to pay for that poor choice. I wanted to feel every moment. I wanted to make sure I made amends in that way. I chose to suffer while that little life was being killed.

Many times since then I have tortured myself with the details of that day. I have relived every moment again and again in my head simply so I would remember the horrible person I was.

That is the interesting thing about shame. Shame loves to torture you by showing you all the ways you have failed. Shame can stop you in your tracks. Shame can prohibit growth. It can make you stay when you should leave. It can make you hurt yourself when you should heal. It can make you reach for a bottle or a drug when you should reach out for a hug. Some shame, however, should not be owned—shame about being molested, raped, beaten, emotionally or physically abused—and the list goes on. However, in its crafty way, shame still worms its ugly way into the hearts and minds of its victims. Most people cannot stop the tape from being played over and over again in their minds. We see this in the multitude of people who lean on drugs and alcohol, who stay with their abusers and lead lives wrought with guilt. Shame removes the fight within and makes you want to hide instead. Shame reduces you to a trembling coward.

My shame was not something that happened to me. Shame was something I chose to accept. Even now I sometimes struggle with shame. For many years I felt I could not be forgiven, and I was unable to talk about my abortion. For many years I told myself I was a bad person. I medicated myself so I would feel nothing. I hid from what I had done. This behavior became an endless cycle and changed nothing. Shame cannot erase anything that has happened. It only binds you in that dark world you so desperately wish to escape. Only the power of God's love and his grace, Spirit, and Word can make a difference. I wish I had known that then.

After the nurse finished taking my vitals and asking her questions, I had to sign papers consenting to the termination and then talk with a psychologist. The psychologist asked me questions about my last period and if I knew what the procedure would be like. Her questions seemed to go on and on. I became irritated. I had made my decision. I wanted to get it over with. Prolonging the procedure only made me think more about my decision.

Then she began some light conversation, and her easy demeanor helped me relax. I started to treat her like she was one of my girlfriends. I asked her about the people protesting outside the clinic. Their judgment bothered me. She told me they were always here on abortion days and not to worry.

"They are hypocrites," she said.

She told me some of those protestors had chosen abortions themselves. Again I felt at ease with my decision.

I left that room and was taken to a different room to get changed into a gown. Then the same quiet, gentle nurse led me down the hall to another room. She opened the door, and I was ushered inside. The room looked like a nicely decorated living room. The nurse told me I'd be called when they were ready. Then I noticed all the faces. Faces staring back at me. Many different women—adults and teenagers from all walks of life—all dressed in hospital gowns, sat around the room. I had not seen another patient until this moment. This was the first time I came face to face with other women who were having abortions.

We were a sober group. No one made eye contact or attempted to make small talk. No one offered a smile or gestured to a seat next to them. I looked around the room hoping to find a friend or someone to connect with to fill the ever-growing void I was feeling inside. But everyone sat in their own personal hell and didn't want company. I noticed that most of the women weren't showing yet. It made it easy to imagine that we were all there for another purpose.

All our chairs faced a TV along one of the walls—as if the clinic were attempting to divert our minds from the task ahead. Like zombies, we watched a game show where the contestants tried to win prizes. The constant sound of laughter and cheering from the exuberant players contrasted with the somber atmosphere of the room.

I lost myself in the mindless game show until the door opened and the nurse called out a woman's name. The woman who stood had to be at least ten years older than most of us and was visibly pregnant—her round belly protruding past her toes. She was the only one among us who seemed to be further along. I caught the eyes of one of the girls in the room and we shared a look. We judged her at that moment. Her baby was a *baby*—not just cells.

Now I realize how mixed-up my thinking was. My thoughts reflected the nature of people. We compare ourselves to others and rationalize our choices and actions, even if we are holding the knife and doing the same thing. I felt justified in my choice because I had convinced myself that my baby was not yet a baby—only cells.

It wasn't long before the older woman came back crying. She

wiped her eyes and nose with a balled-up tissue as she sobbed. Some of the other girls started to tear up, too, and the room started to feel uncomfortable again. Still, no one spoke. No one reached out to comfort her or hear her story. We all had our own stories to tell and needed comfort. I made eye contact with another girl in the room, and although we exchanged no words, our look spoke volumes. We would not cry. We would be strong. We would do this.

The woman continued to cry off and on as we waited for our names to be called. The waiting seemed endless. The cheering and laughing on TV combined with this woman's crying felt surreal.

Later, I learned that this woman had come back into the room because her pregnancy was too far along and she had to have additional procedures for the baby to come out "clean." Thankfully, none of us knew this at the time—although I wonder if it would have changed any of our minds.

A commercial for diapers came on. Beautiful babies smiled and cooed from the television screen. Once more, the TV seemed to be tormenting us. Instantly everyone started to shift in their seats. Some of the girls looked away, and some started to cry. At that point I hardened my heart, took a breath, and watched the whole thing without blinking. I looked at each baby, wondering if the little life inside me would look like the baby on the screen if I would be willing to let it grow.

The nurse called another name and broke the spell. As the girls were called one by one, each stood and walked to her fate. The rest of us held our breath and waited. Before I knew it, my name was called. I stood and walked to the nurse. I looked back one last time at the woman who was still crying. I didn't judge her anymore.

As I walked down the short hallway, I glanced in each room that had an open door. Each looked like a gynecologist's exam room with at least one nurse in each. However, there seemed to be only one doctor who went from room to room. The process felt like an assembly line. He had already visited the first room I peeked in, and the nurse was trying to help the girl sit up. In the second room, a girl was putting her feet in the stirrups. The nurse noticed me and quickly shut the door.

I walked into the last room on the left and immediately had

second thoughts. Pushing my fears down, I remembered all the things I wanted to do and how this baby would affect my dreams. The nurse prepped me and told me to lie back and put my feet in the stirrups. She asked me again if I wanted anesthesia for the procedure, but I was determined to feel the pain of this loss. Before I felt ready, the doctor walked in. He told me I'd feel pressure and the worst cramps I'd ever had.

As he began the procedure, a loud sucking sound like a vacuum filled my ears. The doctor had prepared me for the pain, but not for that noise. Then I felt the instruments go into my body, creating much pressure. The pain was intense—more than I'd ever experienced up to this point in my life. I tried to pull away, but the nurse pushed me back toward the machine. I saw compassion and empathy in the nurse's eyes, but the doctor shook his head as I tried to slide away again. The nurse told me to stay still. I tried to occupy my mind by looking around the room. I noticed a little see-through tube positioned near my knees. The tube was attached to the vacuum and to me. I focused on the tube, wondering if I would see my baby. I knew I wouldn't, but in my pain-filled mind I wanted to see. As tears filled my eyes and rolled down my face, I thought, *I deserve this.*

The procedure ended almost as quickly as it had begun. The quiet in the room was in stark contrast to the noise of the machine that had taken away my baby's life. The nurse gave me a pair of underwear and a sanitary napkin and then took me to a dressing room, where I switched the surgical gown for my own clothes. Once dressed, I was taken into yet another room. In this room was a long table with different papers full of instructions. I gripped the stack of papers they handed me and listened as the person helping me told me I could bleed up to a month. She told me what to look for in case something went wrong. I barely listened as the numbness took hold of my body. Then I was escorted out to the hallway.

I never saw any of the other women again. I sometimes wonder if their stories ended like mine or if they were able to tuck the hurt deep inside and carry on. I even wonder if some did not feel any shame, but simply relief. I know everyone processes loss differently, and I would never judge them for how they processed theirs. I think about the older woman, and I hope the broken piece of her soul has been filled with the love of our Savior like mine has been.

Walking out of the clinic, I felt numb. I had thought relief and happiness would have descended on me, but I only felt . . . nothing. This detachment would last for years as I walked through life like a zombie.

The nurse led me through another door, and I saw my roommate and friend waiting to take me home. They hugged me and asked me how it went. I'm not sure I replied. I just wanted out of there. I wanted to run from this. We opened the door to leave, and I was surprised by the silence. The parking lot was now empty. A small part of me had hoped my mockers would be there to hurl their insults at me. I wanted to feel even worse about myself, but they had left. Having lost the fight for my baby's life, they had put away their signs and verbal abuse and had gone home to their normal lives.

Even after I became a Christian and knew God did not approve of abortion, I still felt unwilling to take the stand these protestors do every day. I felt like a hypocrite and a liar because of my choice. My voice had been effectively silenced on this topic. Although abortion is at the forefront of almost every political race, because of my choice I felt silenced, unable to speak up. My shame drowned my voice until it wasn't even a whisper.

The next month passed by in a blur. I tried hard not to remember anything by using marijuana to dull my thoughts. I remember talking to my parents, telling them I was okay, and crying in the arms of my boyfriend. But I felt alone. Everyone moved on with their lives, but my life seemed to stagnate. Usually I am a talkative person and share too many details of my life with everyone. During this period, though, I couldn't say anything to anyone, and thus remained locked in my own hell.

In addition, my constant pain and blood loss reminded me of what I had done. Within the discharge from my body were pieces of tissue, and I wondered what part of my baby they represented. I cried so much. I had hoped to never think about my choice again, but now I thought about it every second of every day. I couldn't share these thoughts with anyone; I could only keep them inside. As the ugly head of my grief and pain came roaring up to crush me, I beat it back down into the small place in my heart where I let it reign. If the noise got too loud, I reached for drugs or alcohol to quiet the pain.

Outwardly I looked the same. I still laughed and conversed with my friends. I still had fun. But inwardly I struggled to process the shame and guilt. Somehow I finished the term and began packing for home. As I stepped aboard that plane, I was not the same girl who had come to school. My inner being was broken, hardened, and numbed by my choices and my drug use. The excited girl who had won the scholarship and had her whole life ahead of her was gone. She would never fully return. By taking my baby's life, some of my own life had died too.

I sometimes wish I had never had a choice—that I would have been forced to have my baby. I broke the trust I'd built with myself and with God. A piece of my soul is still with that life I chose to kill. God created us together and infused each of us with his essence. When we kill, it hurts that part inside of us. I know my life would not look like it does now if I'd made a different choice then. I struggled with decisions for many years after this, questioning every move. Regret and hindsight always go hand in hand, but God is faithful, and he eventually brought me to a place of peace and love.

Chapter 4

The Aftermath

*Some became fools through their rebellious ways and
suffered affliction because of their iniquities.*
Psalm 107:17

I stepped off the plane and into the arms of my family. Nothing had changed in the way they treated me, but everything had changed in the way I responded to them. My wild and free spirit—including the girl who loved to laugh and wanted to please everyone—had fled. We didn't speak of my choice, but it weighed heavily on every conversation.

That summer I got a job organizing files at an office in my hometown. I spent many hours sorting through paperwork and alphabetizing files. My hands stayed busy and my brain stayed engaged. That job helped me keep my thoughts from drifting toward babies and blood.

My boyfriend and his friends planned to visit during the second month of break and would work in and explore my home state for the summer. When they arrived, my parents graciously welcomed them into their home. I wonder now if I would do the same if I were in their shoes.

As soon as my boyfriend arrived, we fell back into old habits—smoking marijuana and drinking. I felt desperate to redeem myself and my life in some way, and I clung to the relationship. But we started to fight more than we ever had. In hindsight, I know our fights were because a small part of me saw my baby every time I saw him. I blamed myself for what happened, but I also blamed him. His adventurous spirit quickly became bored with my small town, and he wanted to travel and explore. I'm sure our constant fighting also contributed to his desire to leave. No one had a car, so he hitchhiked to a town two hours away. I told him I would meet him there later.

I'll never forget the fight that ensued when I asked to borrow my parents' car, telling them I planned to follow my boyfriend. They wanted me to stay and continue with my job. I grabbed my backpack and started walking. My older brother and his girlfriend caught up with me and offered a ride, only to use that time to beg and plead with me to reconsider. An hour later, I stepped out of the car, and my brother cried. I sometimes think about how hard it was for him to let me go. Any older brother's sworn job is to protect his little sister. Unable to change my mind, he watched helplessly as I slammed the door and hitchhiked down the road.

I spent the next month sleeping in a tent and eating at soup kitchens while finding odd jobs for enough money to feed a drug habit for my boyfriend and me. Although I never used hard drugs, we used a quarter ounce of marijuana every other day. The drug began to affect me more and more, and I sank into a quiet place. Our fights continued. I realized the life we were living was not the one I had envisioned, but somehow I never considered a different path. I thought I had to stay this course to make sense of my decision. By sticking together, I reasoned, it would prove I had made the right choice.

By the end of the summer, I had alienated my friends and family. I became a person no one recognized, not even myself. Close family friends took me to dinner, trying to talk sense into me, attempting to show me that my boyfriend was not the right person for me. I stubbornly defended my boyfriend, desperately clinging to the hope that he would be my redemption.

The month after my boyfriend and his friends came to visit,

he left for Hawaii with his family and invited me along. I willingly went—to escape. I hoped that a different environment would change how I felt about myself. Home reminded me of the person I used to be and how I longed to still be her. Away in another setting, I could pretend I was a whole new person. I hoped the change of scenery would change my hurt.

My boyfriend was still wild and free, unencumbered by my choice. He enjoyed dancing and laughing, partying, and meeting new people—all reasons I had fallen in love with him in the first place. However, now I had changed, and I began to hate everything I once loved about him. Every time he laughed or danced, I inwardly cringed. I sat on the beach one night watching the stars, wondering where I fit in this life. The pain in my heart hurt—despite the beautiful locale—and I didn't know what to do with the ache except to keep burying it deep inside. Anytime a thought, sound, or image triggered thoughts of my abortion, I would spiral into a cycle of grief, shame, and guilt. No amount of gorgeous sun or pristine beaches could change the pain in my heart.

Somewhere amid all this, my boyfriend decided he would change schools. I hugged him goodbye and promised to visit him at his new school, not knowing it would be the last time I would ever see him. I wish I had been able to put my feelings into words. I wish we could have discussed how my choice changed us, but I still felt numb and didn't know how to explain my feelings—not even to myself.

That fall, I walked into my new apartment with my roommates and tried to forget the last three months. I heard from my boyfriend only a few times as he adjusted to his new life. Our conversations were rushed with little being said.

In October, I was in a car accident. I left a message for my boyfriend to call me. It took him a week to return my call. His slow response reminded me of that night with the white stick—the weekend he didn't come back until Monday—and the anger began to build again. When he finally returned my call, I released all my pent-up rage on him, and he hung up on me.

When he called back, I told him if he ever hung up on me again not to call back. We started to argue again, and once more he hung up on me. It was the last time we spoke.

I hit an all-time low in my life after that phone call. I seques-
tered myself in my room and smoked a whole pack of cigarettes,
clutching my bottle of pain pills and wondering if death would
take away my pain. When my roommate checked in on me, she
knew something was wrong and called my mom. My mom immediately called a suicide hotline, and I spent the night talking with
one of their counselors. My mom then hopped on the next plane
to see me and spent a week taking care of me. She walked me to
class, helped me with my medicine, and encouraged me to live the
life I had been given.

I have not contemplated suicide since I understand now how
the darkness of your inner thoughts can hinder any light from
shining through. Once the light is gone, hope is gone.

It was months before I saw the beauty in life again. Months
passed before my smile returned. As I began to see the light again,
another boy started paying attention to me. We quickly became a
couple and started having sex. I had been taking birth control pills
since my abortion, but I also made him wear a condom. I did not
want to risk anything again. It's funny how not having sex never
seemed to be an option for me.

I still wanted to be loved, but I had changed. Although I liked
this boy, my heart was closed off. I could not let my heart be broken
again—I needed to protect myself in any way possible. I guarded
my heart for months. When summer neared, I couldn't keep up the
fight anymore. I didn't want to be in a relationship and try to love
someone. I just wanted to be free.

I decided to take two of my girlfriends home for the summer.
With them by my side, I hoped my heart would finally heal. My
parents, happy I'd brought girls instead of a boy, were even willing
to give us their van to travel. During one of those trips, as I stood
looking into the vast wilderness while my girlfriends slept, I realized I'd missed my period again. I hoped against hope that I was
not pregnant.

I had stopped taking my pills after I returned home, but there
was no way I could be pregnant since my boyfriend and I had used
condoms and I had been on the pill during our times together.
I lived in denial for the next couple of days. My girlfriends and
I spent two more nights camping before we got the call that our

work contracts were being called in. We had signed on to work a month in a remote village where the only way in was by plane or boat. We looked at it as an adventure and a way to make money while doing something we had never done before. We had to report to the airport by noon the next day.

As we were driving home, I decided to tell my girlfriends about possibly being pregnant again. When we were about twenty minutes from my house, we decided I should stop at the store and get a pregnancy test. I walked into a store where I had worked the summer before I went to college. I hid the test underneath a candy bar as I paid. Then I went to the bathroom as my girlfriends waited outside the door—just as my dormmates had the year before.

As I peed on the little white stick, I thought, *This is not happening. You are being crazy.* As the urine spread through the first window and then the second, I watched the first line appear and then the second. Once again, I stared at that life-changing stick in disbelief.

I pressed my forehead into the cold, hard metal of the bathroom stall door and looked down at my girlfriends' feet. Time seemed to stand still again as the quiet permeated the bathroom. I held my breath, hoping to make the moment go away. Then the quiet broke as I gasped and began to feel my anger build.

How could this have happened? I had done what was right to protect myself. Why was this happening to me again? I had spent the last year of my life recovering from that awful choice and the breakup of my relationship, seeking to repair the darkness in my soul with drugs and alcohol. In my mind, I was happy. I was numb, but happily numb. I was passing my classes and had friends who loved me. That summer was meant to be one of renewal, a revitalization of the old me. I was not ready to face this circumstance again.

My girlfriends hugged me and told me we would get through this. We quickly came up with a plan to continue with the contract to work. We would leave the next day for fishing. I told my friends I did not want my parents to know, and we promised to act normal and get on the plane. We arrived home late and went straight to bed. The next morning became a frantic packing session as we tried to ensure we had everything we needed for our month away. The chaos helped me forget my situation. I didn't have time to think about the new life growing inside me. Once again, I pushed reality out of my mind and sought to carry on with my life.

As we were about to leave, I stood in my parents' room saying my goodbyes.

"Have you gotten your period?" my mom asked.

I froze. I have never been a good liar. It makes me sweat and I can't stop talking. I looked at her and said, "No. I'm pregnant." After a quick pause, I added, "Please don't tell Dad."

She looked at me with concern. "What you are going to do?"

"I'll figure it out."

In truth, I hadn't decided. I'd been too busy planning our trip and avoiding reality. I left in a rush, promising we would call.

I am not sure how my mom let me walk out the door. I think about it now as I look at my own daughters and wonder if I would have had the courage to let my daughter make her own choices and walk out the door. My mom never judged me. She simply handled it all with love and grace.

I stepped off the plane in that small town and was driven to a fishing camp a couple miles outside of town. My girlfriends and I were housed in bunk beds, four to a room. We had committed to sixteen-hour workdays and were told our shift would start at 2:00 a.m. and end at 6:00 p.m. The first five days were spent waiting for the fish to come in. We spent the time exploring the camp. Outside the bathrooms was a pay phone we could use to call home. We were repeatedly told that if we missed a shift or were late, we would be fired, and it would be up to us to pay for getting home. Tickets home were over a thousand dollars. We were stranded.

I would like to say I grew up at work camp, that I started making responsible choices. I'd like to say I was willing to sacrifice my future for the little life growing inside me, but instead I did what I was good at—I hid and pretended the truth was a lie.

My girlfriends and I spent the downtime talking about my pregnancy. One of my girlfriends advised getting an abortion; the other did not. I felt torn between the two opinions. Either way, I had decided to stop drinking and doing drugs until I figured out what to do.

I needed to call my boyfriend and let him know, although we

were supposed to be taking the summer off. It was only fair to tell him. Perhaps he'd offer an opinion too. I looked out at the vast ocean and dialed his number. He answered, happy to hear from me—until I told him my news. Then he sounded shocked and started asking me all kinds of questions I could not answer. I told him I would call him again soon and then hung up.

The fish finally came in, and we started working our six-teen-hour shifts. Once again, I became sick. My girlfriends and I worked the same shift, but in different areas. Since I was experienced at working in a fish cannery, I worked on the line separating the different grades of fish. Thankfully, this part of the "slime line" was also closest to the bathroom. The first couple of weeks when I would take off running for the bathroom, no one said anything. My bosses didn't complain because I showed up on time, worked hard, and got the job done—despite my runs to the bathroom. After many weeks of stripping off my outer layers (they were not allowed in the bathrooms) and running to the bathroom multiple times per shift, the rumors started to fly. My girlfriends and I decided to tell everyone I had an ulcer. Most people bought into the lie. No one except my two girlfriends knew the torment I faced.

That month at fish camp, I went from 120 pounds to 100 pounds. My 5'6" frame looked like a skeleton with skin. I have a picture of myself the day I left the fish camp. When I look at it now and peer into the eyes of the lost soul in the picture, I wonder what I was thinking then and wish I could go back and make a different choice. I often have the urge to yell, "Don't do it!" to the girl in the picture.

Although I was still vomiting daily, this pregnancy seemed completely different from the last one. The last time I had been an emotional wreck, but that had only lasted ten days. This time, four weeks passed before I made my decision, and by the end of those four weeks, I had reached my lowest low.

Even writing about it now makes me want to hide from the truth of that time. I know I am not the person I was, but I also know I am a sinner like everyone else. I am capable of evil things. The only difference now is I have God's Spirit inside me, filling me with the fruit of his Spirit. His words of truth are written on my heart. Despite this truth, the Evil One still tries to use my shame, guilt, and fear to paralyze me. I almost stopped writing this book two chapters ago because of that fear. But I hold on to the hope that I may be able to help someone. My motivation is that someone will be helped by my words, that they will not have to go through what I went through. I also hold on to the hope of redemption for someone who has made the same choices and has felt the shame, guilt, and anger I have.

My girlfriends offered comfort and support. My mom's phone calls encouraged me. She also sent me a package of home remedies for the vomiting, but nothing helped.

While speaking with my boyfriend on the phone, he lamented about how hard his life was and how the situation stressed him. Once again, I felt like my other half had abandoned me when I needed him most. I was *living* the hardship and the stress. I lived it 24/7. He was a good guy, kind and caring, but he had no idea how to deal with our situation. We were both young and simply trying to survive an impossible state of affairs. Besides, I had been broken when we met, and I'd never been able to give my heart fully to him.

As time went on, I found myself leaning toward one decision, but I knew this time I could not lie to myself. This baby was more than just a bunch of cells. This "bunch of cells" had, by now, started to form an actual person with hands, feet, and even facial features. I know now that the bunch of cells had been shaped and formed by the Creator. He had breathed life into them. His or her soul was already there, inside me. God had already created a purpose and a plan for their life, but I would still choose to end it.

The day before my girlfriends and I left for home, I decided I would once again abort my baby. I celebrated that decision by smoking marijuana again and going to the bar to drink for the first time in four weeks. My reasons were different this time. I reasoned my partying and drug use would have somehow messed up the baby. I didn't want the baby to suffer in this life with physical deformities or mental incapacities, so ending his or her life before it started seemed like a good thing to do.

As I write this now, I can't help but to be dumbfounded by this way of thinking. These thoughts had nothing to do with the baby's well-being, but had everything to do with my own selfish desires to not be inconvenienced by a damaged baby. I knew my life would forever be tied to this baby's father as well. I knew he would want to be part of the baby's life. But I knew I did not want to be tied to any one person. I had grown too numb to think of anyone but myself.

Throughout the last month of our job, my girlfriends and I had made friends with the guys in the bunk room next to us. We had spent time in their room hanging out, and everyone smoked pot except me. One of the guys paid special attention to me. I think he saw the broken part of me and, being broken himself, was drawn to that brokenness. Our relationship started off innocent enough. He shared a funny story or a kind word, and I laughed or smiled. I was desensitized to my feelings at this point, but appreciated someone being willing to want to take care of me. He wrote me poetry and left me homemade gifts—birds made from paper. The attention flattered me. His attentions helped me feel normal. He had a sweet smile and beautiful eyes. As we left the fish cannery, I said we would meet up again, but I never told him my secret.

Chapter 5

In the Darkness

Some sat in darkness, in utter darkness, prisoners suffering
in iron chains, because they rebelled against God's
commands and despised the plans
of the Most High.
Psalm 107:10–11

When I returned home, my mother made me tell my father. She didn't want to keep the secret from him. I was angry—angry at myself, the situation, and that I was making this choice again. Unlike before, I knew I would not come out of this unscathed. In my mind, a bevy of irrational thoughts abounded. How could I have a baby after aborting one just a year earlier? How could I tie myself to this man I didn't even love? I was not ready for the responsibilities of these choices. Yet I knew my soul would simply fracture wider with the decision I was about to make. But because of my fear and shame, I trudged on like a solider marching to defeat.

The conversation with my dad the next day only increased my anger and made me hate myself more. At the time, my parents did not know the right words to say, and I don't blame them. They did what they thought was best. I could not begrudge them their hurt, anger, and disappointment in my choices. It had to be incredibly difficult to watch the daughter they raised continually make painful choices.

Two days after returning home, I turned twenty-one, and my family took me out. We went to dinner, where I had my first "real" drink, although by then I'd had many drinks. Even though they knew I planned to abort this baby, too, I don't think it made it any easier for my parents to see me drinking while pregnant.

My friends were leaving soon and we wanted to go out one last time, so I kissed my parents goodbye and left with my friends. Once again, I simply wanted a normal life. I wanted to act my age, to party and have fun. I had already moved on, but it was different for my parents. I can't even imagine what they must have been thinking as they watched me ignore the baby in my belly. The fact that they loved me through this time is a testament to their unconditional love for me.

My friends and I went to our local bar and met up with the boys we had bunked next to at the cannery. I laughed and allowed everyone to celebrate my birthday, all the while denying the little life inside me. I saw my sweet-eyed poet and began to pound down the alcohol. I drank four Long Island Iced Teas and a shot of whiskey within a few hours. It proved to be too much for my 105-pound frame, and I blacked out.

When next I woke, I was being dragged out the back door of the bar by my friends. They told me I'd been sick multiple times in the bathroom. Then I threw up again outside. My friends dragged me away to the beach where the boys had a tent. The rest of that night is blank for me.

The next morning, I woke up in the poet's tent with the urge to once again vomit. I ran out of the tent and emptied the contents of my stomach on the beach. My poet ran after me, concerned. I told him I was pregnant.

As his eyes widened in surprise, I felt the shame and guilt build once more in my gut.

I had reached the lowest point in my life. I was twenty-one, more than eight weeks pregnant, still drunk from the night before, and couldn't remember if I had slept with a boy I had met only a couple of weeks ago.

Years later, when I wanted to torture myself, I'd force myself to remember this moment on the beach. I'd remember the sad look in his eyes.

Once he'd recovered from the shock, the poet gave me his number and we promised to talk. I'm not sure if it was out of pity or if he really cared. I ventured home—still drunk—vomiting most of the way. For the next three days, I could barely leave my bed except to be sick. My girlfriends tried to be supportive, each in their own way, and I appreciated their friendship, but there was nothing they could do for me. They decided to head home.

A couple of days later, my mom left with my youngest brother to visit family on the East Coast, and my dad and a friend left to go fishing. Their trips had been planned weeks in advance—they would not change them for my bad decisions. And I didn't blame them. I'd gotten myself into this situation, and I had to deal with it alone.

One day while everyone was gone, I hitchhiked to a nondescript building in a tiny office park on the other side of town. This time I encountered no protestors. No friend accompanied me. No one tried to change my mind. There was no receptionist, no music, and no aquarium. I am not sure if there was even a waiting room. Only a doctor and a nurse.

This time when asked if I wanted the drugs for the pain, I said yes. Having medicated myself the whole last year to numb my heartache, I felt desperate to blunt this pain too. I remember two things. One: being alone. The nurse asked me if I had a ride home. I said no. She looked at me with pity in her eyes and then ended up driving me home after the procedure. Two: the ultrasound the doctor did before the procedure. I watched his eyes and thought I saw sadness or anger there. Perhaps I was projecting my own emotions. As he moved the device around my belly, his hand stopped, and I knew he had found what he was looking for. I wish I would have asked to look. It haunts me to this day that I did not see that baby. Tears fill my eyes as I write this. The hurt runs deep.

The nurse drove me home. I took a shower and went to bed, hoping sleep would transport me to the land of peace.

After this abortion, I didn't even try to hide how broken I felt. I moped around the house, spent a lot of time in bed, and alienated everyone, including good friends. I bought drugs and smoked them by myself, often disappearing into the woods to spend many hours staring endlessly into the vast forest, wishing I could disappear. I was not the same person anymore. In fact, I knew that the carefree girl I'd been before my abortions would never return. My choices had affected every aspect of my life and had now destroyed it. I sat in a dark place.

When my mom returned from her trip, she demanded I attend counseling. I appeased her and saw a counselor one time before I returned to school. During that one session, I told the therapist—without tears—everything I had done, how I felt about myself, and that I was using drugs (mostly marijuana) and alcohol to medicate the pain. She encouraged me to stop that behavior and gave me a one-day-at-a-time coin. I promised to try.

When I returned to school this time, my life felt empty. To protect myself, to be able to move through the motions, I shut down my emotions. I locked them up tight within. I felt more than broken—I felt destroyed. In this dark place, I could see no light, no hope.

I contacted my poet and returned to school early to stay with him, trying desperately to cling to something—someone. I needed light, a savior, an escape—someone to make me feel loved and alive. My poet had spoken sweet words to me and had given me tokens of his affection before. I hoped for freedom and love once again in his arms.

He took me to his family's house next to the ocean. The island where he lived spoke of the quiet beauty that refreshed my soul. I met his parents and spent time with his happy, loving puppy. We didn't talk about my choices or what had happened, but instead simply enjoyed each other's company. We had sex on the first night of my stay. I no longer felt a hesitation in giving myself away. I needed something to make me feel whole and loved—to fill the void within.

I never connected the anguish, shame, and guilt I felt to my sex life. In my mind, my pregnancies were something that happened *to me*, not something I *chose*. I still used birth control and condoms, but kept making one bad choice after another. I sought the light, but in all the wrong, dark places. I tried to find my savior in the arms of a mortal instead of seeking the one true Savior. When you expect another human being to fill the void left by our Creator, you will never find the light.

Their house, situated on the end of an island along a small bay, was a beautiful, warm, and welcoming home. My boyfriend's parents were just as inviting. Of course, they did not know my dirty secrets. I wonder if they would have loved me as much if they had known.

Every day, I sat in a rocking chair on the porch overlooking the bay and watched the sunset. My boyfriend's music would wash over me as he played different melodies on his piano—some his own. A quiet, gentle beauty spoke to me. In those moments, I knew there had to be more to life than what I was experiencing. I longed for a different life, a better life. In that chair I heard the stirrings of my soul.

The poet showed me his town. We went kayaking, met his friends, and went to festivals. All the while I carried my dark secrets and heartbreak. His beautiful golden retriever easily gave me his love. He followed me around and wagged his tail. He loved my poet, but I think he sensed the deep hurt inside me and tried to comfort me too. I think about this time now and see how God was working to bring me closer to him—already courting me with his creations like the sunsets and this beautiful dog. But I did not think about God then. God's gift of forgiveness couldn't possibly extend to me while I sat in this dark place. I would not have accepted forgiveness at that point, even if it had been offered. My God had to spend time healing me in small ways first.

The time spent with my poet became an escape for me, but he was chased by his own demons. When I returned to school, we tried to make the relationship work, but it ended just as quickly as it started. I am still grateful, however, for his willingness to give me a lifeline—a small pinprick of light—at that low point in my life.

Back at school, things had changed for me as well. My previous boyfriend was now friends with some boys who had once been my friends. They were now his roommates and hated me. Our group still hung out together, but I was no longer welcome. This loss felt like another dagger to my heart. I had introduced him to my friends, and now he had been accepted, but I was not. I felt alone and heartbroken. I hardened my heart and turned once again to drugs and alcohol to combat the feelings.

One day I looked in the mirror. The woman looking back seemed a hazy reflection of my former self. The wide, innocent, and mischievous eyes had been exchanged for hardened, untrusting, bitter ones. My once-long hair had been chopped off. Instead of the honey-kissed blonde, it was now a hard red. My teeth were no longer white, but were stained yellow from all the cigarettes I smoked. I had lost the plump cheeks of my youth and had harsher features due to the corrosion in my soul. There was nothing innocent, nothing pure in my face, but only emptiness. I preferred to be alone now, but still partied to ease the pain, not to spend time with friends. I didn't care, and it showed. I kept up with schoolwork, but I couldn't keep a job. I felt lost. I had met new friends but had no interest in boys. It was an empty life.

Most of my junior year was spent going to class, making new friends, and partying. I found myself doing things I never thought I would do. One night a girl I'd met in one of my classes decided we'd go out with a friend of hers. My friend and I had made a pact to stick together. I reasoned nothing too bad could ever happen to me if we were together.

We ran into a friend of my friend at the party, he was a cute guy and super nice. We all decided to go have drinks at a strip club—some place I'd never been. The place assaulted my senses. The music was loud—louder than any club I'd been in, almost as if to drown out the groans of the men and the shame of the women. The walls were decorated with red and dark wood to try to make the place look classy, but it felt dirty and had a sickly plastic smell. Smoke from endless cigarettes created a haze that almost softened the harshness of this place, but everywhere I looked, I saw flesh. Everywhere I looked, eyes followed me. The women were beautiful, but seemed lost, like me. I wondered what had driven them to work in this place, wondering if the shame they struggled with was like mine. I did not want to give my power over to a man like they were doing, though—letting men leer at them and throw money their way. This dark place began to open my eyes to what my life could look like if I didn't find the light. After a while we decided to leave the club, and we ended up driving him home. He had beautiful eyes. He invited us in. My friend had to be somewhere the next day, but I wasn't ready to go back to my empty apartment. My friend encouraged me to stay, so I jumped out of the car and went in with him. The man and I spent the night talking, laughing, and making out. When the morning came, he drove me home. No other man I'd met had a car, his own place, made his own money, or had his life together as this man did. He felt like a breath of fresh air, and I made a place for him in my life. I didn't understand then that I was simply still trying to fill that void that only my Creator could fill.

Chapter 6

Turning Point

Some wandered in desert wastelands, finding no way to a city where they could settle. They were hungry and thirsty, and their lives ebbed away.
Psalm 107:4–5

Bringing this man into my life brought a calm that hadn't been there before. He proved to be a good friend to me and a "nice" guy. He showed me the importance of finding friendship in a relationship and not just fleeting feelings. He had his life more together than any of the other guys I had dated, which brought me a sense of peace. However, he liked to party just as much as I did. I began to compartmentalize my life.

In my schooling, I worked hard in my classes to obtain good grades and excel at learning. In my personal life, I partied, acted wild, and had fun. On the outside, I seemed like a normal young adult. On the inside, I was a mess. Occasionally the different compartments I'd set up for myself bled into one another, and the strain of keeping my secrets and how I really felt about myself mixed.

My life began to be about spending time with my new beau. He loved sports, and we spent most weekend days watching them. At night we partied. We had a group of friends who hung out together and cooked elaborate meals. I have great memories of spending time with them. Even though things seemed good on the outside, I still used drugs and alcohol to combat the feelings of shame and guilt I carried on the inside.

Although I felt conflicted inside, I still wanted to try new things. Perhaps I wanted to try to fill the hole with activity. In the summer between my junior and senior years, I decided to try a summer-abroad program through my school. I would spend three weeks with other students and teachers at a sponsor school forty-five minutes outside of Amsterdam. I used my scholarship money for the trip.

Within a day of settling into our dorms, our host school hosted a dinner for us. As we walked into the beautifully arranged dinner at the end of the pier, I noticed the bottles of wine. It would quickly become apparent I was the wildest one in my group.

On each table were two bottles of wine. These poor Europeans didn't understand American youth and alcohol. They kept serving us wine every time we asked. Our table of ten cleared six bottles of wine before the first course was even served. Soon I was wasted and strode over to the table of advisors, teachers, and the president of the host school. I spoke to them in a fake European accent. One of my teachers said I should probably stop drinking, and I agreed. I blacked out shortly after this conversation, but somehow made it back to my dorm.

I am grateful everyone extended grace to me that night and that my school did not send me home. Even though I was of legal drinking age, I represented the school—and I had done so poorly. They had invited me into their school, and my thanks was to abuse alcohol and embarrass myself. This school had given me so much—including a scholarship—and I acted like a fool. I often wonder if my teacher had sensed how lost I was and simply extended grace to me during this time. I was also thankful I had once again been taken care of while blacked out. It is obvious to me now that God was protecting me, even when he was the furthest thing from my mind.

The person I am now is so far from the girl I was then. Thinking about it now makes me cringe. I always hesitate to engage when I find someone who went to school with me, afraid I may have done something they would remember, but I wouldn't. Many nights I woke up in strange places and didn't remember anything.

Now I can see how God was preparing my heart for him. This trip showed me there was more to life than my own backyard. I discovered a whole world with so many cool things to see. My teachers were amazing. They wanted us to experience Europe fully and planned all kinds of excursions. We toured art museums, churches, government buildings, graveyards, and the international courts. When we visited the Anne Frank house, I felt sickened by the stories of the children killed by the Nazis. I wondered if I was just as bad as them because I'd killed my babies too. I still had nightmares and flashbacks of the blood, pain, and anguish I'd felt, but I kept pushing it down, attempting to live a normal life.

Looking back now on this trip, I wish I'd been aware of how amazing it was, but my focus remained on numbing my pain. Despite all these amazing experiences, I could not be fully present because that would require acknowledging the hurt hidden inside and just below the surface. Even though I loved exploring the new countries, tasting the new food, and seeing the new sights, I remained numb.

The school week was only four days, and we had the weekends off to do what we wanted. We walked the streets of Amsterdam and saw people shooting needles into their arms and bellies. Looking down an alleyway, we saw people cooking up heroin. The scene was crazy to see, even for me, and tugged on something inside me. I had never shot up—it scared me. Even though I felt like I'd ruined my life, I did not want to chase the dragon. Seeing these people and their lifestyles so vividly and the lengths they'd go to for their drugs made me pause. The girl who had left for college all those years ago was gone, but her essence wanted to come back. She just couldn't find her way.

One weekend, a group I'd made friends with decided we wanted to find harder drugs to try. We went in search of mushrooms and "E." I had done Ecstasy a handful of times and loved the feeling. The euphoria I felt made me forget all my pain, but the drug left a nasty hangover and tremendous head and teeth pain. This drug also gave me a false sense of love for myself and everyone around me.

We quickly found the drugs—it wasn't difficult in this city. However, when we didn't start feeling the effect right away, we continued to smoke marijuana and drink. When the effects finally hit, it was not how I'd remembered. I felt a lot more mellow than usual and more peaceful. We went to a party to hang out with the other kids from the program, and I talked to all different kinds of people. Laughing and dancing, I had the time of my life. As the night wore on, I started to randomly vomit. However, after I'd gotten sick, I'd continue talking to whomever I'd been speaking to before. I shudder now to think what those people must have thought of me.

At one point I took a guitar from one of the guys and proceeded to play it in front of everyone. I had never played a guitar before, but I suddenly felt like a pro. I became lost in my own song. Turns out I was simply lost in the false feelings only drugs can give you. When you fully lose yourself to those false feelings, they take over, and you do and think things that do not represent you. Although I felt as unhappy as ever, I acted happy and seemed to be having a good time. However, the drugs were only masking my pain—like putting a Band-Aid over a gaping chest wound. The guilt, shame, and hurt all still lingered inside.

After I returned to my dorm that night, I lay on my bed, unable to go to sleep. Each bedroom room had two beds with a short wooden wall separating them. I watched cartoons for half an hour on this wall before I realized there was no TV, no cartoons. This moment scared me. If my brain was doing this, there was no telling what other damage I was doing to my body. It was the first time since my abortions that I thought about protecting and fighting for myself.

I decided I no longer wanted to do hard drugs and did not want to damage my brain. I knew that if I continued down this path I would die. Dying meant meeting God, and I surely did not want to face God at this point.

About two weeks into our trip, four of us decided to take an extra week to backpack around Europe by ourselves. We planned to backpack through Germany, the Czech Republic, and Austria. One of the guys had brought his best friend, and he ended up meeting another girl, so there were six of us total. We had our final dinner with our host school—they wisely did not serve alcohol that night—and I was able to hold myself together and say goodbye.

Before I had left for Europe, I learned that Europeans like to be stylish and cared about what they wore. Instead of anything practical, I had only packed my three-inch platform shoes. I hiked across Europe in those, with a forty-pound backpack I had traded my suitcase for. Each night one of the guys in our group would wash and dress my blisters. Good thing we drank enough alcohol every day to numb that pain too.

I have a flash-card memory of my experiences that week. A symphony at the top of the mountain. Touring a castle. Walking down a bridge in Prague. In every instance I was either drunk or in the process of getting drunk. I remember drinking absinthe—a dangerous mix of high amounts of alcohol strained through woodworm leaves. The liquid burned as it made its way down my throat, but then the fun, happy, wild Jackie would emerge. I vomited in every country we visited—on the side of the streets, on the train, in various bathrooms. I think our group could have been the poster children for the "dumb" American college kids the Europeans complain about.

Our group slept in hostels and trains together, and we bonded. We took care of each other—at least in the most basic sense. I felt like I belonged and was doing something amazing. The trip helped me forget—at least for a little bit—all the hurt and pain of the last few years.

On our way out of Germany, we all got food poisoning. Most of us were on the same plane coming back to the States and boarded still feeling sick. When we deplaned, customs officers—seeing what looked like hungover college kids—decided to do a detailed search of our stuff. Not surprisingly, some of our mementos had traces of drugs on them. They took us to a back room where we were searched more thoroughly and then questioned. We were fortunate that they let us off with only a monetary fine.

I walked right on the edge and tried very hard not to fall, but came close several times. I had been on the cusp of disaster many times, but somehow it always brushed by me. I don't think it was luck. I know now God had a plan. I didn't deserve his redemption or his grace, but he gave it anyway. He had a plan for me that didn't involve death or imprisonment. Although those things certainly could have happened, his protection never faltered. Some people whom I partied with in college are now in prison or dead. I know I could have been one of them.

At the time I was doing all these things, I did not think about God or his plan for my life. But he was thinking of me! I didn't see it then, but there is always hope. That beacon of light comes from the Holy One if you will only seek him. He is the one who infuses hope into our souls. He knows our sin, and yet still chooses to have a relationship with us. When you are faced with a hopeless situation, turn to God.

In my senior year, I was required to spend a term working as an intern. I chose a company that fit my lifestyle—they sold tie-dyed items at concerts. The man who ran the company was smart and driven. He gave me free rein to do a marketing research project to determine if the in-store promotions were helpful to their end users. I loved not having someone looking over my shoulder. My project was successful, and I was promoted to marketing.

Next, I sought to redesign their trade-show booth and marketing tools to showcase their products at the national trade-show. Going over the plans and seeing the different design ideas for the new booths thrilled me. I was able to plan and present everything related to the trade-show—all the giveaways and the entire design. My boss let me call most of the shots without my even asking him for direction. The owner and I liked each other, and the company asked me to stay on.

I thought I was maintaining my life and succeeding—yet I'm now not sure how I accomplished all these things while still taking drugs. I appeared to be doing well, but I still didn't feel happy. I left a trail of broken promises and disappointments behind me.

I still did not feel whole. I still longed to fill the break in my soul. I still tried to numb that space with drugs and alcohol. My college years were coming to an end, and I would have to decide what I wanted to do next. School gave me a purpose and focus. Once it was over, how would I cope?

I ended up working for this company and settling into a more sedentary lifestyle. Instead of going out to party every night, I found coworkers who liked to smoke marijuana, and we did so after work in a more relaxed atmosphere. One of my coworkers was an interesting older guy who had toured with bands and traveled all over the world. We connected and enjoyed spending time together. We began to work on the trade-show project together.

We flew to the trade-show a day early and were in the middle of trying to get things set up when my boss called to ask questions. I did not have time for his interruptions and became impatient with his questions. He, in turn, became annoyed with my lack of answers and became more demanding. When he asked to speak with my coworker, I said we were too busy and hung up on him.

Looking back, I realize I acted naïvely and arrogantly. My boss had given me free rein and trusted me with big projects, but I did not give him the respect he deserved. I couldn't see this disrespect at the time because I was doing too many drugs. My arrogance had always come across as confidence. At the lowest points of my life, I relied on my arrogance and false bravado to get me through. This time was no different. I pridefully thought I didn't have to answer to him. In addition, I ended up getting drunk and saying very disrespectful things about him in front of him and many others. At the time, I thought nothing of it. Looking back, I know this was the beginning of the end for me. He had given me so much trust and freedom, and I had abused it.

I was entering a new phase in my life. I would be done with college in February, but would walk with my class in May because of my summer in Europe. I planned to work at my job and figure out what to do next.

Then my great-grandmother died.

My nana, although sharp-tongued, had always been special to me. She told me she loved me all the time and was also an incredible seamstress. Every Christmas of my childhood, we would get homemade stuffed animals, and the labels had her name on them.

I remember getting a pink elephant that I have to this day; my own kids now cuddle that special toy.

My nana's passing was another step on the path that God had laid out for me. My great-grandmother's death helped me realize that life is short and we only have a set amount of time. When someone you love dies, you think about your life and your priorities. Once again, I thought about dying and meeting God. I was not ready for that interaction.

Seeing my family also made me feel more like the girl I used to be—the girl I wanted to be. That trip reminded me there were people who loved me and wanted to look out for me. My great-grandmother's death was a sad time for our family, but it sparked a sense of belonging in me. I left my grandparents' home sad, but wanting more from my life.

After Nana's funeral, I returned to my job and was fired. At the time, I was angry and didn't understand why I'd been let go—they needed me, after all. The fact that I'd disrespected my boss never crossed my mind; I had never considered the consequences of my rudeness. I had taken the job and my boss's trust for granted. More failure. I felt embarrassed and ashamed. I wanted to lash out. Instead, I ran.

Losing Nana and my job changed my mindset. I had to get my life together. I had nothing holding me to my life and lifestyle anymore. I felt like a failure and had to escape these feelings.

As I walked out of my job with a box of all my paperwork and with tears streaming down my face, I looked up. A gentle breeze brushed my face. I knew there had to be more than this—more than the disappointment my life had become, more than the bad choices I had made, more than my shame, guilt, and fear. There had to be more. I didn't know what the more was at that time, and I didn't know how to find it, but I knew I had to stop using drugs to medicate my pain.

I knew I was not strong enough to say no to the drugs and the partying while still hanging out with my friends, so I decided to visit my uncle who lived in southern Florida. He'd offered to let me visit when we'd spoken at the funeral. I was on a plane within a week of losing my job.

My boyfriend and my friends felt shocked and confused by

my departure, but I was desperate to get away from my life. I had to clean out my mind. I needed to find the real me again—to face the me who had made those horrible decisions to kill my babies. I felt the waves of transition crash through my life and knew this was a turning point. Although I didn't want to face my internal turmoil, the alternative—continuing to fail and numbing myself with drugs—no longer held any appeal. I booked a ticket with no idea when I would return; I just had to escape.

Sometimes in life you must step away. I don't see it as running away, but consciously taking a step away from your environment to obtain a new perspective and insight on what you are doing and what you want. Running away implies not coming back. Stepping away implies you will eventually return—you just need time to process. I had spent the last four years doing things I said I never would, making one bad choice after another—choices that defined how I felt about myself. I did not know how to escape those feelings. Had I not stepped onto that plane to Florida, I truly believe my life would have continued in the same direction for many more years. Now I am grateful that my boss fired me. I am also grateful that my aunt and uncle took me in and did not ask any questions. When I arrived on their doorstep, they happily embraced me. They simply took me in and loved me. I am eternally grateful that they were willing to do so.

My aunt's life revolved around horses. Before I knew it, I was helping her out at the barn. My aunt and uncle did not have children, so my aunt and I quickly bonded and had a lot of fun together. A driven, hardworking person, she even let me try on her wedding dress. I am grateful for my aunt's friendship and insight.

My uncle had a wild side and understood some of what I was going through. I came to them with nothing, broken, not knowing what to do. Yet they loved on me. They fed me, housed me, and hung out with me—and asked nothing of me. I am so grateful God put them in my life. They seemed to know I needed help. Their home became a place of refuge. I stepped away from my old life because it was not what I needed anymore.

However, the pain I felt as the result of my abortions did not end. My wounds had sliced a jagged cut deep in my soul that had only been bandaged by drugs—not fully healed. Although I now felt secure with my aunt and uncle, without the drugs my thoughts began to overtake me once more. Those thoughts—once kept at bay—turned into overwhelming feelings of disgust. All the horrendous things I'd done replayed over and over in my head, resulting in the familiar feelings of shame and guilt coming once again to the surface. In the past, I'd reached for drugs to combat these feelings. While at my uncle and aunt's home, there was no easy fix, and for the first time I had to combat these feelings without any "help." I began searching for something more—some real relief.

Another aunt and uncle lived nearby, and I spent time at their home too. They equally loved on me, but their lives were a bit crazier, having two daughters both under the age of three. I loved getting lost in the chaos of their home—it distracted me from my negative thoughts. Seeing the little ones did not trigger any feelings of resentment or shame, but rather I fell in love with their sweetness and innocence.

During one of my visits, my aunt and uncle asked me to join them at their church. My gut reaction was to say no, but I said yes because I didn't want to disappoint anyone else in my life.

We attended the Wednesday night service. Inside were hundreds of people singing and swaying to the music. At first, I was taken aback. It felt weird because it was so different from the more solemn service of the Catholic Church to which I was accustomed. Everyone had a Bible and sat at a long table in a school cafeteria. I was only familiar with my mother's big white Catholic Bible with the lace and the gold edging and a picture of Mary and Jesus on the cover.

Before I left for college, I had taken some classes at the Catholic Church and had been confirmed. The couple who'd taught had a King James Bible, and we were able to read some things from it, but I could not connect with the words. A few short months later, I renounced my faith and my God, deciding that the universe was made up of energy and we were the gods.

Now I sat on that cold cafeteria bench and watched everyone singing joyfully to a God I didn't believe in and who I thought abandoned sinners such as myself. The worship group seemed less structured than the Catholic Church, and the music was different from that of my youth, but the words spoke to my soul. I watched people embrace each other with joy. People opened their Bibles and read the Word of God without any hesitation. They seemed so happy, warm, and friendly. Many came up to me to say hello. I felt defensive, but intrigued. My curiosity was piqued.

My uncle shared with me his journey of coming to the faith, but I countered what he said with my Catholic upbringing. I didn't know you could speak directly to God or that you could have a relationship directly with the Lord rather than through Mary or the saints. As we spoke, the church members began splitting off into different groups. Someone asked me if I wanted to go to the newcomers' group. My uncle said I could stay with them if I wanted to, but I wanted to see what this church was about and, I think, also wanted to prove them wrong. As everyone got up to find their group, I made my way through the hundreds of people and found the group of newcomers.

A man sat us in a circle and had us each introduce ourselves. Then he said a prayer and began to talk about God. I vividly remember one passage of Scripture that he read—Hebrews 10:26–27:

> If we deliberately keep on sinning after we have received
> the knowledge of the truth, no sacrifice for sins is left,
> but only a fearful expectation of judgment and of raging
> fire that will consume the enemies of God.

For the first time in my life, I felt a burning in my soul. The first words of the Scripture spoke truth directly into my being. I knew that having the abortions had been wrong and sinful. I knew most of the choices I had made after that had been wrong too. I knew that up to that point, I had not only been doing sinful things, but I had also been *deliberately* making those choices. I had *deliberately* kept sinning, just as the verse said.

Of course, no one likes to be told that what they are doing is wrong, and I was no different. I felt my defenses go up. Then the next part of the Scripture scared me. Even though I had been living this nightmare called my life, I had only started thinking about my future within the last month. Now the group was discussing heaven and hell—our next life. If I continued on this path, according to this Scripture, judgment and raging fire waited for me. My mind continued to whir with this new information as I listened to the leader talk about the consequences of our sins. *Why is he trying to scare me? I want help, not condemnation.*

As soon as the class concluded, I accused the leader of trying to scare people into going to his church and accepting Christ. I boldly refused to look at my sin, and I accused him of manipulation. Instead of arguing with me, the man simply walked away.

To this day, I wonder about his reaction. How did God know that's exactly the kind of response I needed at that time? If this man had engaged with me, if he had argued with me, if he had tried to speak the truth to me, I would not have been open to his reasoning. We would have simply argued. Instead, he walked away, taking away a bit of my fight. That Scripture continued to resonate in my soul. I realized if I died right then, I would go to hell. Although I was not ready to forgive myself or to accept God, this moment became the starting point for my healing.

As I left the church that night, my uncle gave me a Bible, and I accepted it. It was a small black hardcover NIV version—the first Bible I'd ever received. When I opened the Bible to Genesis, I read the story of creation. It finally made sense to me. This story had been taught to me many times, but I had never read it for myself. Now the words and truth came alive.

God opened my heart to him that night. I began to seek him every day. I read Scripture and then discussed it with my aunt and uncle. The more I read, the more the Lord opened my heart. He pursued me. He spoke his words to me, and they resonated within me. He opened my broken heart and fractured soul and poured his living water into them.

God opened himself up to me in such a way as to capture my heart. Even now there are days when I open my Bible and am amazed at how much his words fill me.

But the process was slow. I was not ready to commit to anything or anyone—even God. By the time my stay with my aunt and uncle was coming to an end, my numbness had lessened. My heart had grown soft. I sought more for my life.

I still hadn't fully accepted God, but I knew there was more to my life than what I had been living. As I hugged my uncle goodbye, I told him I had left home searching for something, and now I knew I had been searching for God. When I arrived home, I started attending a sister church.

I met a vibrant, loving woman at this church who would become one of my best friends and a spiritual guide for me. She, along with two other women, started studying the Bible with me, helped me know more about God, and pursued me with their love and friendship. I loved my college friends, but I did not have any who didn't party. These women were different. They showed me a side to life I hadn't experienced in over four years. We laughed, cried, and had fun together without drugs or alcohol. I began to relearn how to live life in a healthy way. I had been lost in the darkness for so long that it took God, this church, and these women to pull me out.

I came home a different person. Although still filled with shame and guilt, I wanted more from my life. I had killed two babies, but I wanted healing and redemption. The ultimate Healer and Redeemer didn't disappoint. While I sat in the heart of my sin and darkness, God was making a way. He looked for me and prepared the way for me to accept him. He knew I needed him. He knows you need him too. He offers another way—not always an easier way, but one filled with light and love from our Creator. Seek it, and he will find you and redeem you too.

At my graduation, I walked across the stage with a clearer head than I'd had the entire time I'd been in school. The next day I left with my family for a family reunion, which turned into another amazing moment in God's plan for me. Everyone in my family is loud, a bit wild, and funny. This reunion was no different. As I talked, laughed, and was loved, some of my wounds began to heal. I felt connected to something outside of the drugs. I felt supported.

I came back from the reunion ready to learn more about God, but the next couple of weeks were hard. I had to come to terms with the thought that all sin is the same, although the consequences are different. I had to believe God would forgive *my* sins. I felt I deserved my punishments, and it took me a while to accept God's saving grace. It would be many years before I was ready to forgive myself. The shame and guilt crippled me at points, but I was good at compartmentalizing, and I put those two tiny babies in a box in my heart and closed the door.

One night, my friends from church asked me to write down every sin I felt I had committed against God and others. Then they asked if I was willing to read my list to them. Reading that list out loud took a measure of trust in them and in God in order to lay all my ugliness before them. Writing my sins and reading the list out loud convicted me that I never wanted to do any of those things again. I knew I was ready for a new life. I knew God had forgiven me. A burden had been lifted. I was no longer hiding. I had confessed and brought my sins into the light.

I decided to accept Jesus and got baptized on the same day— June 20, 1999—Father's Day. What a perfect way to express my love for my God, my heavenly Father. I ended my college years by making the most important decision of my life. I was still broken. I was still filled with shame. I was still fearful. However, now I had the love of my Savior, and that love gave me the freedom to once again pursue dreams.

Chapter 7

God's Love

*In a desert land he found him, in a barren and howling
waste. He shielded him and cared for him;
he guarded him as the apple of his eye.*
Deuteronomy 32:10

Before I could fully embrace my new life, I had to give up
the old. This meant moving out of my apartment where I
had used drugs and partied with my friends. When I went there
to pack, all I could see was drug paraphernalia. The items I'd used
for my drug habit, empty beer cans, full ashtrays—every item embarrassed me. I had taken two guys from church along to help me
move, and now they were seeing all my dirty secrets. As they gath-
ered up the few things I owned, I tried to usher them away from
my old life. I made eye contact with one of the guys, but I saw no
judgment in his eyes.

That summer I spent most of my time on people's couches
while I tried to figure out what to do. I needed to find a job and
develop a life plan, but more than anything, I needed to heal. Even
though everyone was kind to me, I felt lonely. I kept busy with

tons of activities and fun events. But in the quiet times late at night or early in the morning, I still felt alone. In those moments, the ugly demon of shame haunted me. The demon told me all sorts of things about how I wasn't good enough, how I deserved to be lonely, and how I didn't deserve to be accepted. He enjoyed beating me down and making me feel unworthy. I began to read Scripture after Scripture about the love and grace of our heavenly Father. These words became a balm to my heart. I began using God's precious words to counter the ugly thoughts.

My brothers and sisters in the church taught me how to live a godly life also—how to shut out the demons. One of the married couples I met offered to let me live in their basement while I figured out my next steps. They allowed me to be a part of a functioning family and removed the pressures of living on my own. I found a job working at a bank in the human resources department, where I had to dress up every day. While I hated being attached to a phone line, I loved helping people understand and get the most out of their benefits. I worked hard. It was the first job I'd had since being on my own where drugs were not part of my life.

I started making friends and participating in church activities. I tried to keep some of my old friends, but their lifestyles were now so different from my own. Although I'd been raised a Christian, I still didn't have a relationship with God. However, now I was willing to give up everything—including the friends who I felt had been there for me—to follow my God. Having found him, I wouldn't let anything take him away this time.

Then I had the dreaded abortion conversation with my new Christian friends. One new friend started a discussion by saying, "Abortion is so wrong. I'd never kill one of God's children." She, of course, did not know my history. Looks of judgment and condemnation passed around the group as each person nodded their agreement. I felt the shame and guilt burning deep within. Part of me wanted to defend the women, like me, who had reasons for their decisions, but now I knew my choices had been wrong. Part of me wanted to stay and listen to all the judgmental things they said about abortion, simply to torture myself again. Instead, I said nothing and walked away. Their statements—their opinions—hurt deeply. I buried them in that secret place within my soul. Those dark feelings stayed hidden until the Spirit prompted me to bring them out once again.

About four months after becoming a Christian, I finally shared my abortion story with one of my new friends. She confided to me that she'd had one too. I asked how she felt about her abortion and what her thoughts were now. She said she didn't think of it at all. "You have to forgive yourself and not think about it," she said. God had forgiven her, and she had accepted that truth.

Her statement amazed me.

I wasn't *trying* to think about it; I *tried* to hide it away. At the time, I thought that if I forgave myself I would be denying my sin. I would never let myself off the hook for those sins. I owed both those babies at least that much.

After talking to my friend and seeing how she felt about her abortion, I started talking about my abortions to more women. I had never considered that others also held this deep pain. I wanted to connect with those women, to find a place of belonging and understanding. In our church of three hundred, I spoke with at least five women who'd had an abortion. Every single one was young when they had unprotected sex and got pregnant. None had wanted a baby at the time. However, not all of them felt like I did. Some felt that as soon as they were saved, they were able to forgive themselves and move on. Some, like me, were carrying shame and guilt. Some had never talked about it with anyone but had buried it deep. Some are still lost in the guilt. Although some know they are healed from their sin by the saving grace of God, they never forget. At the time, choosing abortion may seem like choosing freedom, but it will bind your soul, for abortion is a choice that can haunt you for a lifetime.

However, one of the most awe-inspiring things about God is that he knows your inner thoughts, plans, dreams, and wishes. He knew where I kept my secret hurts and pain and my deepest desires. He knew what I longed for and needed before I ever did. As

God dug me out of the pit I had created, he helped me remember my dreams and deepest desires. He gave my dreams back to me.

That following April, the church leaders asked me if I would go to a meeting to learn about being a missionary in Albania. I immediately said yes. I had always said yes impulsively, jumping into things without thinking them through. This time, though, I hoped saying yes would be for the greater good.

At the meeting, we learned about the poverty from lack of jobs and the hopelessness of a people who had been oppressed by their government. We also heard stories of how willing these people were to hear about God. Their open hearts longed for the Savior's words. As I watched all the slides and heard about these beautiful people, I became inspired. I wanted to help.

The trip would be a one-year commitment, and we'd leave in one month. Fifty of us attended that meeting, but only ten were chosen to go. A few days later, I was notified that I'd been chosen, and I quickly began to prepare. I had so much to do to put my life on hold while I took a year off. I had to move everything into storage, sell my car, and ask my friends to care for my cat. My parents were not happy. They had just gotten their daughter back, and now I was flying to Albania—a country with a history of violence and unrest. I had changed so much in the last year, but my parents were skeptical that I had really changed. I hardly trusted myself. But when something is God's plan, it works out. So with as much bravery as I had when I left for college, I finished packing, said goodbye to everything I knew, grabbed my two suitcases, got on a plane by myself, and flew across the ocean.

The team was made up of about twenty people from various countries. They were a mix of married couples, single men and women, and one family with two children. The married couples had already been in Albania for a few months, and the church was experiencing rapid growth. Although some had never heard the Bible—it was outlawed under the communist regime—the Albanian people were open to God. Seventy percent of the country claimed to be Muslim; however, most were nonpracticing.

I strode off the plane at the little airport ready to win hearts for Christ. A fellow team member met me. We grabbed my two bags and took a taxi to the city, which was half an hour away. I watched the strange scenery pass by. The country was dusty; everything looked dirty. Many guards walked around with huge guns—so different from the streets of America. The buildings were mostly made of concrete. Countless animals—mostly dogs and cats—roamed the streets. Many looked sick or hurt. Then I noticed the people. Young, as well as old, looked sick and broken too. I wondered what had happened to them. As we exited the taxi, I noticed the smell—a mixture of animals, people, and raw sewage.

I dropped my bags off at the apartment I would be sharing with the other single sisters and walked to a restaurant to have dinner with the team. Excited to be there and to be following my dream, I thought nothing of what I was putting in my mouth. The next morning as my stomach rebelled, I quickly learned that public toilets are mostly an American concept. However, the Albanians are gracious people, and I was able to plead with business owners to use their bathrooms, which consisted of two porcelain footsteps and a hole in the ground.

We often got sick from the food. No Food and Drug Administration ensured its safety. The electricity would be on for only a few hours a day in the wintertime. Sometimes the water was available only once a day. We never drank the water because it felt like glass in your belly. Albania was unlike any place I had ever been.

As we walked around the city the next day, we were given a brief overview of the dangers of Albania. We were told, as women, never to use a taxi, because we could be easily driven to the country and raped. We were told to always travel in pairs, and never go into the house of someone we didn't know. We learned that the city we were in was part of the sex-traffic highway.

I heard strange music throughout the day, but did not know what it meant. Then we learned that the music was from the mosques calling Muslims to prayer.

Some of the people I'd seen earlier were street children. Young kids around the ages of five or six that had been forced to leave their homes to find food. They joined gangs and had to sell cigarettes. I called them the cigarette boys. If they could not sell enough, they were beaten. Whenever I could, I gave them money. It was hard to see the brokenness of this country. I cried for their suffering. The heartbreak was a raw, daily experience for the people and animals here. People were starving in the streets, taken advantage of, and used for profit. I felt hopeless and overwhelmed.

I realized early on that the only thing I could offer them was the hope of Jesus. This became a time of great personal growth in my relationship with God. The couples on the team who led the church had been Christians for a long time and offered me much wisdom. I wanted to learn God's ways, and they were able to teach me.

The trip was both physically challenging and spiritually amazing. It changed my whole worldview. I no longer took things for granted, and my thinking about how to live my life changed drastically. I became grateful for what I had. The experience showed me I had been blessed to have been born in the United States, and it also showed me a beautiful people who had bad circumstances but good hearts.

I fell in love with the Albanian women and their beautiful spirit. They had no concept of personal space, but I loved how close they would walk with us. I came to appreciate their culture—so different from our own. I spent the year unlearning my American culture and learning theirs.

Our leaders challenged us to read the Bible cover to cover twice that year. We began by reading a couple of hours a day. In my reading I began to see the heart of God and the sin of the people. David's life story made me feel better. Even though he had really messed up, God still called him a man after his own heart.

In February, I was chosen to go help a church in Macedonia. For the first time, I had started dating a Christian. He was one of the single men on the mission team. He would accompany me. We were assigned to relieve the couple who was leading the church there. The church was small and the people were not as open as the people in Albania, but I made friends and tried my best to encourage them with Scripture and God's love. I had more time on my hands than I normally did during this time. This country was not as poor as Albania, so I indulged in luxuries I hadn't had in six months—namely fast food.

About three weeks after arriving, I was reading about Paul. I wanted to be someone who was thought of as Paul was—a true and faithful servant of God. So I prayed an arrogant prayer. I prayed that God would test me as he had tested Paul. I wanted to prove my faithfulness to God as Paul had. I even went so far as to pray that God would not hold back. I had no idea what I was asking for. I simply prayed this prayer and went about my life.

Within a week I was on a plane to Greece due to unexplained abdominal pain. I ended up spending many days in the hospital getting poked and prodded. Most of the nurses did not speak English, and they put things in my IV that made my arms numb and warm. After having a colonoscopy unlike any we'd consider "reasonable" in the States, I was flown to the United States for surgery. Due to the horrific hospital experience in Greece, I have since struggled with two autoimmune diseases and countless other weird symptoms and sicknesses. It was one of the scariest and loneliest times for me. Like Paul, my health became an ongoing thorn in my flesh.

After spending a month with my grandparents, I flew back to Albania to finish out my commitment, but everything was different. I had been gone for four weeks, and in my absence things had changed. Besides, I felt that by being gone I'd failed in my commitment. That May, I flew back home. The familiar shame and failure that I had tucked away for the past year followed me there.

I was sad to leave the Albanian people, but was happy to be home. However, so many things were different now, and I faced a huge adjustment period. I had loved the secluded world of the mission field where all I had to worry about was God and helping people. There had been no bills to worry about and no need to figure things out for ourselves—everything had been planned and organized by others. Returning to the states and to a place that held so many memories of my failure proved difficult. I had spent a year in a bubble, but now I had to start planning a future for myself. I stayed at my parents' home awaiting my brother's wedding as I slowly adjusted. I started reacquainting myself with my friends from high school. I was not the same girl who'd left, but was closer to my old self.

A test I'd had in the hospital before leaving Albania had come back with negative results. I had to go see a doctor, and it was determined I would need surgery. This would be my second surgery in three months, and it started to wear on me. I went from having a purpose to having none. I went from reading my Bible for hours at a time to reading it for only minutes a day. God was answering my arrogant prayer about being challenged, and it took a toll on the patchwork bandage I had put on my scars.

During the next four months, I started drinking wine daily and going out with friends. I had worked so hard in Albania and was tired. I'd had two surgeries and still wasn't feeling the best. I deserved this break. I deserved to feel good. This mindset led me to meet up with an old high school boyfriend. I decided to travel with him and another couple to meet up with a friend in another town. In hindsight, I should have stayed away. I should have seen the danger signs as I slowly started walking away from God and his way. I still had a deep hole of hurt in me. Instead of maintaining my relationship with God, once again I thought I could heal that hurt with a boy.

My need to be loved and adored was still part of who I was. I was still broken. I had yet to forgive myself, so I had this need to be fulfilled and accepted by someone else. I needed to have someone love me because I did not love myself. This boy told me beautiful things about myself. He said he had always loved me and that I was a good person. I didn't correct him, but fell in love with him all over again in one night.

I couldn't have imagined a more romantic love story than this. As we drove back from hanging out with our friends, he shared his feelings for me. During this heartfelt speech, an amazing thing occurred. The northern lights, which are rarely seen in August in Alaska, came out in full force. The sky was filled with beautiful green and purple ribbons of light dancing for our entertainment. At the same time, we must have been having a meteor shower, as tons of shooting stars filled the sky.

I thought God was telling me this boy was special. I wonder now if this spectacular moment was simply God trying to help me to remember him before I chose to do something I regretted.

We spent that night and the next day together. When I returned home, my mom told me she was worried I'd gone back to my old ways. I didn't listen. Instead, I decided to be with this boy even though I knew doing so went against God. The morning after I spent the night and day with him, I awoke in my bedroom and took out my Bible.

I fanned out my Bible and stopped at a random passage. I had determined that whatever Scripture I landed on was what God was trying to tell me. (Sometimes I still play this game with myself, but now I try to remember to keep God's Word in context.) I looked up and said, *Okay, God. If you want me to change, you need to tell me.*

I landed on 2 Samuel 12. In this chapter, the prophet Nathan points out David's prior sins—lusting after Bathsheba and murdering her husband—and calls him to repentance. I knew the Scripture before I read it, and I looked up at God shaking my head. The message seemed crystal clear. God was telling me I couldn't have both my relationship with this boy and with him. I had to choose, just as David had. I could either continue in this sin, or repent and come back to the Lord. I could have chosen to repent later and stayed with my boyfriend. I'm sure he would have been faithful and, perhaps, even loved me for a good while. But I knew there would be consequences. A broken trail of consequences—the results of poor choices—littered my past.

This was one of my hardest decisions as a Christian. I didn't want to leave this boy, but I knew I had to choose. I left to fly back to Rhode Island the next day. I knew if I decided to forsake God in that moment by staying in Alaska with this boy, it would have worn away my relationship with God. I had come back from the mission field a hero in the church's eyes, and yet I had still committed an intentional sin against God. Although God had already forgiven me and I had chosen him, the consequences of this not only hurt me and God, but they also hurt the boy. God had rescued me and saved me, and I had betrayed him. I knew these choices had been the result of my renewed drinking and the brokenness I still felt inside—the brokenness that God had forgiven, but that I was unwilling to let heal.

I decided to take part in Chemical Recovery, a substance abuse recovery ministry that was starting at my church in Rhode Island. The leaders told us to journal about every time we had used alcohol or drugs, write how much we'd used, how it had made us feel, and what the consequences had been. This was the first step in helping me process my time in college. I started with the first time I smoked a cigarette as a ten-year-old and then wrote about all the times I had drunk alcohol or done drugs—all the way up to my last time drinking wine that summer. At first, I indicated that I'd felt happy or that it had been fun, but I was challenged to look deeper. As I started to really think about those incidents, the strongest emotion I felt was sadness. Everything after my abortions—all the times I'd used drugs or alcohol—was due to sadness, fear, anger, or shame. But mostly, I was sad. Sad that I'd lost my innocence. Sad that I hadn't stood up for myself. Sad that I had chosen to terminate my pregnancies. Sad that I had hurt people. Sad that I had lost myself in the process.

Now that I had defined what I felt, the feeling draped itself around my spirit. I hate to cry and rarely cry in front of anyone. Even to this day, I usually drive around and cry in my car by myself. My husband has rarely seen me cry during our marriage. However, during this time the tears flowed freely. I grieved for myself. I grieved for all my bad mistakes. I grieved for all the people I'd hurt.

It took me months, but I graduated from the program and haven't taken another drink in fifteen years. I didn't trust myself. I still don't. I know that no matter how much I think I can handle the situation, there is always part of me that knows how easily I could fall. I protect myself from myself. I try not to put myself in situations where it would be easy for me to go back to my old ways. For me, this is the biggest consequence I've had to face since choosing abortion—I don't fully trust myself to make the right decisions. Thankfully, I now have a great group of women, my husband, and God to rely on.

After the recovery program ended, I felt like I'd finally accomplished something good, and I started to process my feelings. Since I'd chosen to take the life of both my babies, the shame and guilt had eaten away at my soul, causing me to make one bad choice after another. When I chose God instead of the drugs and alcohol, I began to find forgiveness for the things I'd done. I still had a long way to go, but now I was beginning to understand God's love and how I could truly forgive myself.

Chapter 8

A New Heart

*I will give them an undivided heart and put a new spirit
in them; I will remove from them their heart of stone and
give them a heart of flesh.*
Ezekiel 11:19

Almost a year after I had left Albania, I realized I was lonely and wanted to start dating. Until this point, I had decided that relationships were not going to be a part of my life. I had failed every relationship I had started, either by hurting someone or getting hurt. Love seemed to be something I no longer deserved. However, God had been working on my heart, and I felt the need to at least pray about this situation. I prayed that God would make it clear if there was really someone special waiting for me. I began fasting so I could truly hear God's words when they came.

Within two days, I heard from one of the boys who'd helped me move. We'd spent New Year's Eve together that year before I left for Albania, but I hadn't heard much from him since. During our phone conversation, he expressed his feelings for me. His words shocked me. My girlfriends had told me he'd gone through a rough patch after I'd left, but he'd never asked to hang out with me and had spent the better part of the year ignoring me. I thought he had moved on. I certainly didn't think he liked me in any way, even though I was always somehow drawn to him. He was charismatic, funny, and handsome. But I was broken and still didn't trust myself. And I was afraid—fearful I'd make the wrong decisions again. I already had a million regrets and didn't need any more. I wanted God to lead me this time. I told the boy I would spend time with him, but I'd make no commitment.

We started directing a play together for charity at our church. I saw him several times a week and regularly talked with him on the phone. Although I enjoyed our conversations and being with him, I was still unsure and feared making the wrong decision. In October, I told him a relationship with him wasn't going to work out. We had to continue working on the play until December, and now when I saw him there was no easygoing chatter, no fun, no laughter. He became silent and short with me. I was hurt and confused. Then I started praying and talking with girlfriends about what to do. Had I made the right choice?

One of my girlfriends said, "You will know if he is the one if you can't imagine not seeing him every day, if it isn't easy to envision your life without him." I thought about what she'd said.

One night after this, he and I got into a fight because I told him I was hurt that he was treating me differently. He said he couldn't treat me the same because it hurt his heart to do so. I left crying. As I drove around a park, I prayed to God about why I couldn't let down my walls. I wanted so much just to be happy. I looked up to God and said, *I want him, I choose him.* Suddenly it was as if my walls came crashing down. I was in love with this man and knew he was meant for me.

Later, I took him out to dinner and told him my feelings. I told him I understood if he wasn't willing to go on my crazy merry-go-round again. He said he was glad I had changed my mind. We spent the rest of the night talking and laughing. He invited me to meet him for lunch two days later. I happily met up with him, and he surprised me with a box of mementos from every date we had been on during the last four years. He then asked me to be his official girlfriend. To say it overwhelmed me would be an understatement. His actions amazed me. Who was I that this man would spend so much time remembering me?

The next six months were filled with many laughs and long conversations. We imposed strict limits on our physical contact and did not even kiss for a while. Song of Solomon 2:7 comes to mind: "Do not arouse or awaken love until it so desires." I knew from my history that once the door to a physical relationship is opened, it cannot be closed. I did not want to ruin this relationship with sex too soon. Placing a physical barrier between us allowed us to get to know each other first. We talked about common interests and shared feelings and values. With him, I felt like I finally fit. I'd found someone who understood and cared.

Six months after we started dating, we were sitting on a beautiful beach. As the waves crashed against the shore, I felt a peace I hadn't felt in a long time. He pulled out a book he'd made with all our memories, experiences, and pictures. At the end of the book was a story written by Robert Schuller entitled, "Saving the Broken Pieces." The story recounts the construction of the world's most beautiful mosaic in the Royal Palace of Tehran. As originally designed, the architect specified huge sheets of mirrors for the walls. When the first shipment arrived from Paris, the mirrors were shattered. The contractor threw them in the trash and delivered the sad news to the architect. The architect ordered all the broken pieces collected, then he smashed them into tiny pieces and glued them to the walls to become a mosaic of silver, shimmering, mirrored bits of glass.

The end of the story says:

> Broken to become beautiful! It's possible to turn your scars into stars. It's possible to be better because of the brokenness. It is extremely rare to find in the great museums of the world objects of antiquity that are unbroken. Indeed, some of the most precious pieces in the world are only fragments that remain a hallowed reminder of a glorious past. Never underestimate God's power to repair and restore.[1]

"You make my broken pieces beautiful," my new boyfriend told me. "Will you marry me?"

Tears sprang to my eyes. I laughed and screamed and then said yes.

After calling our family—he had already asked my dad for my hand in marriage—we started planning an October wedding. We would continue to wait until we were married to consummate our marriage. We put God in the middle of our relationship and trusted in him to guide us.

As our wedding date neared, a married couple started mentoring us, encouraging us to talk about our past with each other. I was scared my fiancé would decide to end things once he knew I'd had two abortions. I sat stone-faced and told him about my past, expecting to see a look of disgust cross his face. Instead, I saw understanding and compassion. I did not feel judged by him. He wanted me, and nothing would change his mind.

This is the power of God's love for me. He took my broken and ugly self, unable to crawl out of the dungeon I had made for myself, and picked me up, cleaned me, and provided one of his trusted sons for my husband. I am forever grateful to my loving God for providing this partner. Though far from perfect, he has always been my biggest fan and my best friend. His love for me has allowed me time to heal.

My husband and I decided to wait a while before having our first baby. This was a hard time for me as I went back and forth between wanting a baby and knowing my earlier choices may have hurt my body's ability to have babies. I prayed and journaled a lot during this time. My shame spoke to me, telling me I did not deserve to get pregnant. Being barren would be a fitting consequence for me. But God knew what he wanted for my life.

About four years later, I went to my doctor for some pain I'd been experiencing. They determined I was pregnant. Then, because I'd experienced this pain in my side, they wanted to know how far along I was and wanted to do an ultrasound. They couldn't find the baby and feared I was ectopic—having a pregnancy outside the uterus. About a week later, I started bleeding and had to have

another ultrasound. Unlike the ultrasounds with my first two pregnancies, I wanted to see the picture on the screen this time. This
time, I did not want to escape or wish these cells away. I wanted
this baby. I now longed to be pregnant. I had prayed for this. This
time I was not alone. My husband and sister-in-law sat in that
darkened room with me and eagerly waited to see the flicker of that
tiny heartbeat on the screen. As soon as I saw that little heartbeat
flicker, I fell in love with this tiny soul God had given me. I already
had a dream in my mind for this baby—hope in what he or she
would become.

I didn't spend a lot of time thinking about the first two lives I
had taken anymore. I had perfected tucking those memories away.
If any thoughts or images came to my mind, I pushed them out.

I bought a book that showed all the different growth stages
of my baby. I waited and waited for my belly to grow so everyone
would know. I knew this baby was a blessing from God that I didn't
deserve, but would cherish. I didn't want to hide anymore.

Nine months later, God blessed me with an energetic, smart,
creative, beautiful baby girl.

I had never seen anything more beautiful. My baby had a perfect face. I know now that even if she hadn't been healthy, I would
have loved her just the same. She had come from my body, but had
been formed by God. She was a part of my husband and me—connected to us forever. I was in love with her.

The first year was crazy, as every first year is for first-time parents. The days were hard and the nights long. I decided to be a
stay-at-home mom. At the time I hadn't realized this is the hardest
job one can have.

On my daughter's first birthday, I found out I was pregnant
with my second child. Nine months later I had another beautiful daughter—an exact opposite of her older sister. While my first
daughter was energetic and impulsive, my second was quiet and
thoughtful. She never cried and always seemed laid back. Generous
and kind to a fault, without her my life would have lacked sweetness.

One day I looked at my two beautiful girls and thought about
the two babies I had not given the chance to grow. I wondered
who they might have been today. When I was pregnant then, I'd

told myself those babies would ruin my life. What a lie! Looking at my two daughters now, I knew it had been a lie. I had thought my life would be over. Not true. I had thought I wouldn't be able to accomplish my dreams. Not true. Sure, my life would have looked different and wouldn't have been easy at all, but many other women have raised babies alone. They paved the way in showing other women what it looks like to choose to have their babies. They became single moms and made it work.

I have not met one woman who has regretted choosing to have her baby. Once their baby is placed in their arms, most mothers' love overflows and covers a multitude of worry and regret. I know their lives aren't easy, and they may need to let go of or postpone some dreams. However, every woman I have met who has chosen to have her baby has fallen in love with her or him at first sight. As soon as that baby comes out of our womb and into our arms, we become fiercely protective, and unparalleled love comes over us. We are willing to sacrifice whatever needs to be sacrificed for life.

I know now the lie I told myself would have been proven wrong if I would have had the courage to keep my babies. It would not have been easy, and I would have had to sacrifice some things. But stop for a moment and ask yourself these questions: What in life is easy? What in life is perfect? What in life goes our way all the time? Are there not dreams we must give up to follow God's plan? Is trying to have control of our lives—even though we really don't—worth taking someone else's life? These are questions I encourage anyone who is thinking of abortion to ask themselves.

Now I had two beautiful little girls. Life was crazy and hard. I wondered if I would ever sleep again. I nursed those babies and let them sleep in my bed. I hated to hear them cry and would hold them until they fell asleep. They filled up my every minute, and I felt grateful.

When my second daughter had just finished her first birthday, I found out I was pregnant for the fifth time. The news came as a complete shock to us, but I had made a promise to myself that once I had become a Christian, I would never be upset by a pregnancy again. Instead, I determined to be happy and grateful. I never wanted to go back to the feelings of fear and regret I'd had during my first two pregnancies. If God was willing to bless me, I would be happy.

I looked at that little white stick this time without an ounce of fear. I ran to tell my husband, and we laughed. We had both said we'd been thinking about wanting another baby.

I had my first ultrasound at seven weeks, and again I saw the flicker of the tiny heartbeat—the representation of new life, a new soul. Looking at that heartbeat, I felt a mixture of wonder and horror. I knew that twice before I had decided to still a heartbeat just like this one. The life growing inside me had been terminated for no other reason than my selfish fears. I had always thought of myself as brave and courageous, but in my heart I knew I had been ruled by my fear. I had been a coward. Despite trying to live a life without regrets, I'd made that choice, resulting in two of the biggest regrets of my life.

This pregnancy turned out to be much different than the other four. I started off sick, but the nausea gradually decreased. My sensitivity to food lessened. I no longer wanted to kill anyone who drank coffee near me. I could stand the smell of meat. I thought for sure these things meant I was having a boy. I went to my twelve-week ultrasound full of excitement. I waited with anticipation while the technician put the gel on my belly and moved the probe around searching for my baby. I watched the black screen for the flicker of a heartbeat. Round and round the technician swirled that ball over my belly trying to find a heartbeat. Seconds ticked by and the energy in the room started to feel awkward. She wasn't saying anything, so I asked, "Shouldn't there be a heartbeat?"

She looked me in the eye and said, "Yes, but there isn't one."

The ultrasound technician determined the baby had stopped growing at around seven weeks, right after my last ultrasound. Tears filled my eyes and poured down my face. I knew I deserved this. All the dreams I had had for this life were gone. He or she was at the beginning of their life and had already become a big part of mine.

The old feelings of shame and guilt came back. I felt like I deserved this loss. Although I cried, I didn't get angry or upset. I simply felt this baby's death was justification for the other lives I'd taken.

The tears I cried were tears of want and need. I barely had time to register what had happened when the technician ushered me out of that room and into another. I called my husband and my mom. My husband, who works over an hour away, dropped everything to come home. My mom, who had come to visit and was with my other two kids, told me she would come and meet me. She didn't want me to be alone. I told her to stay with the kids.

The obstetrician wanted me to a schedule a D&C for the next day since my body had not miscarried the baby. I signed the papers and waited for the appointments to be made. Sitting alone in that room, I felt like I did when I'd had my abortions.

As I drove home, I let all the thoughts of my past run through my mind. I was not angry, just sad. I talked with God and knew he was not punishing me, although I felt like I deserved this loss. I could not be mad—I had two beautiful babies already. But I could be sad.

The next day I returned to the hospital with my husband. After the doctor ushered us into the room, I asked for another ultrasound. I had to make sure this baby was gone. I did not want to take another life.

The procedure and aftereffects were just like my abortions. I needed to recover physically, and certain hormones had to leave my body. The only difference? Instead of being riddled with guilt and fear, I felt sad and defeated. I studied God's Word and cried out to him. After my abortions, I had used drugs and other men to ease my pain, but with this miscarriage, I clung to God.

I grieved and said goodbye to that little baby, but my busy life went on. My husband and I didn't try to have another baby, but one morning, six months after my miscarriage, I found myself staring at another little white stick. I found my husband, and we laughed together again. Another unexpected little one. We were shocked and didn't even know how it could have happened—famous words for many couples.

This time I felt both happy and overwhelmed. I had put the desire for another baby to bed and thought that dream was gone. I was content with what God had given me and did not think I was worthy to ask for more. Boy, was I wrong about how our God showers his love on us! By now, I had been pregnant or nursing for over four years. My body had just rebounded, and I was looking forward to the next stage of life. But I'd determined never to be sad about a pregnancy again. As I laughed with my husband, I started to dream for this little one too. I was sick the first month with this pregnancy, as well, but then the nausea abruptly stopped. I knew something was wrong. I called my midwife. Reluctantly she saw me the next day. She told me that everything was fine and that I was simply fearful due to the last miscarriage. But I knew.

I insisted on an ultrasound, and thankfully, she agreed. Again I lay in a dark room—this time with one of my daughters on my chest—watching the ball going around and around in circles on my belly trying to find that tiny heartbeat. Again we looked at a blank screen and saw the mass signifying my baby, but without the flicker of life. There was no heartbeat to be found. The midwife apologized to me, and we scheduled another D&C. This time there were no tears. I simply felt numb and angry. I was not angry at God, but I was angry that I had to go through this loss again.

I walked the familiar pathway into the hospital and operating room. I requested an ultrasound again—just to make sure. I kissed my husband as they wheeled me back for the procedure.

I struggled with thoughts of retribution. I knew from reading God's Word that he would not intentionally hurt us, but he does allow things to happen to bring us to repentance. I felt like I was being punished for many things—for the many bad choices I'd made.

After the D&C, I learned this baby had been another little girl. I sometimes think about what it would be like to have three girls, and I feel sad about what could have been.

After this miscarriage, I gave away all my baby stuff. I decided I needed to clean it all out to start over. I was done being pregnant. I started birth control and tried to move on. I began thinking more about my four dead babies. I continued to feel that my two miscarriages were somehow payment—retribution—for my two abortions. It made sense to me. My friends and family told that was not the way God worked, but my shame and fear told me otherwise. I struggled through his Word and continued to pray, but tried to stay busy and bury the feelings once more. Once the hormones left my body, I started to wonder what my next step would be.

The following spring, I began reading *Kisses from Katie* by Katie Davis Majors. In her book, Ms. Majors speaks about all the hurting and forgotten children in the world—all the suffering they endure. It broke my heart to read this book, but it sparked a desire I had put to rest many years before—adoption. I had watched a show about Haitian girls being mistreated, and my heart longed to rescue one. When I had talked about adoption previously with my husband, he'd said he didn't think he had the heart to adopt. I knew we both had to be on the same page, so I had put that dream away too. Now, after reading Majors's book, the desire to adopt sparked in my heart again. I started praying that if it were God's will for us to adopt, he would change my husband's mind.

One afternoon, after having prayed about this for many days, I asked my husband about adoption again. His answer surprised me.

"I've been thinking about it too," he said.

I took this as a sign that God had a plan for us to adopt. I started reading and researching many kinds of adoption. The possibilities overwhelmed me. My husband and I had many questions to pray over. You can start the journey, but God determines the steps. I spoke to various friends who had adopted, and I obtained advice about how they'd gone through the process. Eventually, after much research and many phone calls, we believed God wanted us to adopt from the United States. We decided it was important to preserve our birth order, which meant finding a child under the age of two.

Many decisions come with adopting a child. Some people look down on people who only want infants. Somehow there is a ranking order on how good you are based on what kind of child you adopt. In the end, you must listen to what God and your inner self tells you. It is a hard but beautiful journey either way.

By February we had decided on an agency, and our friends were having a fundraising dinner for us. Two weeks before the fundraiser I was staring at another little white stick in a drugstore bathroom. I had missed my period and had decided to buy one of those life-changing sticks. Instead of waiting to go home, I had used the bathroom inside the store. My husband was in the car outside, and we were on our way to a marriage retreat without the kids. I looked down at the little stick, and, for the seventh time, two little lines appeared. I was pregnant again. I walked out of the store shocked, but with a smile of disbelief on my face.

However, I hesitated to let my excitement grow because of my two previous miscarriages. I told my friends and the adoption agency we were going to put everything on hold to see if this pregnancy would work. As time passed, I tried not to put too much hope in this baby. When I saw the heartbeat on the ultrasound, even then I guarded my heart. I became super sick and struggled to manage my family life while feeling so awful. I called my mom in Alaska, and she came to help me. Women who've never experienced morning sickness or continued fatigue throughout their pregnancies are fortunate. If you have never been sick in your pregnancies, then you are very lucky. I have been very sick and lost weight during the first trimester of each pregnancy.

This time I was physically sick and emotionally unprepared to be pregnant. My dream had been to adopt and never be pregnant again. As I lay in bed one night, I wondered who this little person would become.

As this pregnancy progressed, I noticed subtle changes from my pregnancies with my girls. I felt different, which led me to believe I was having a boy. At the eighteen-week ultrasound, we saw the outline indicating a boy. My husband cried.

Our son came into the world with white hair and beautiful blue eyes. He was perfect. I laughed when I saw him and praised God, wondering how God could love me so much. My rainbow baby was more than I could have asked for. Although it saddened me to put our dreams of adoption away, and I wasn't sure I could handle four kids, God had known our desire to have another baby. As we trusted him and journeyed toward what we thought he wanted, he'd shown us another way. He always has plans for us. If we are willing to seek and trust him, he will not disappoint. To this day, I look at my son and am overwhelmed by God's love for me.

Six weeks after giving birth, I was packing up our home to move. The day before my son was born, we were told that my husband's company was giving him a promotion, but we'd have to move from Rhode Island to Nashville. I had lived in Rhode Island off and on since I was nineteen. Now in the middle of this great blessing, God was asking me to leave everything and everyone I had known behind. My friends and family had become my security. They had become my source of joy and love. I felt heartbroken and overwhelmed.

Slowly, through all my trials and victories, God was training me to trust in him. He was helping me to understand that if I followed his ways, he would take care of the rest. I was beginning to trust him and have faith in his plan for my life. As God sent Abraham off to an unfamiliar land, he was sending me off too. We responded faithfully to God's call.

We packed up our life and left our friends and family. With three kids under the age of six, I was busy. I had spent the last six years filling myself up with life, but not with God. I still spent time with him, but I wasn't reading my Bible as I should, and our relationship had grown stagnant. I was not making God first in my life. I still held on to some shame for intentionally choosing to sin against him. I knew he had forgiven me, but forgiving oneself is hard. And I often wasn't willing to do the work.

My husband was on a journey of his own. We both loved God, but had demons in our past we needed to deal with. However, life once again intervened, and we both switched into moving mode instead.

Until we could physically move, my husband would be commuting to work in Nashville from our home in Rhode Island and would be gone for a week at a time. There were so many details to manage, and I would be left alone with three young children—including a newborn—and tasked with the packing. During those few weeks, I could feel God pushing me to rely more and more on him.

I told my husband repeatedly how important it was to me that I be at our house with the movers to make sure they packed everything correctly. The morning of our move, I awoke with side pain. Ten minutes before the movers came, I told my husband I needed to go to my neighbor's house to see if they would take me to the doctor. The pain intensified as I walked. When I stepped into their house, I yelled for an ambulance. My neighbor came rushing downstairs to find me on the floor vomiting and in agonizing pain.

My husband came to the hospital with my son so I could nurse, and we waited for the test results. Eventually it was determined I had passed a kidney stone. After giving me some pain medicine, the doctors sent me home. My husband and I had missed moving day. The control I wanted to have over the situation had been stripped from me, and there was nothing I could do but wait and trust in God to make it work.

Because I needed control of *something*, I chose a date—February 21, a random Thursday—to focus on. I needed an end time when I thought all the craziness related to the move would end. I kept my eyes focused on that date, not on God, and hoped things would get better then.

Thursday, February 21, started off clear and beautiful. I had high hopes for the perfect day I had envisioned. Life was still busy, but the house was unpacked and the kids were adjusting. I missed my friends, but we had found a church. As I was dropping off my daughter at school, one of my first friends, and the director of the school, advised me to watch the weather for tornadoes tonight. I was dumbfounded. What did she mean? I had never lived in a place where tornadoes were a threat. I didn't know what to do or expect. She gave me a quick lesson on what to do and not do. I walked away shell-shocked.

I called my husband, who expressed equal surprise. We decided the closet under our stairs would be the safest place in case of a tornado, but prayed we wouldn't need to make that decision.

As we went about our day, we put thoughts of tornadoes out of our heads. That night after dinner we decided to go out for ice cream to celebrate making it through the move and my February 21 date.

As we pulled into the driveway, the storm began. Lightning lit up the sky and thunder rumbled, but I didn't think much of it. We had kids to put to bed and TV to watch. My husband took the kids upstairs to brush their teeth, and I started on the dishes. As I was scrubbing the sauce from one plate, I heard a siren. It sounded like something I'd heard in World War II movies and documentaries when places were getting bombed. Dumbstruck, I stood at the sink, not moving until the wailing made sense to me. A tornado was coming!

Complete chaos ensued. Frantically, we grabbed the kids and tried to fit all five of us in the closet underneath our staircase.

Unpacked boxes, books, electronics, and a vacuum crowded our way. I clutched my eight-week-old baby and my little girls' hands as I prepared to be blown away.

The woman from church had said that a tornado would sound like a freight train bearing down on the house. I listened intently for that sound while nursing my baby.

The storm was loud. Many times I squeezed my eyes shut and thought, *This is it!* only to open them and realize we were still in one piece. My girls cried in fear. They then began saying they wanted to go home to Rhode Island. I started saying it too. My husband tried to find a news station on his phone to see what was happening while we sat in that closet with my kids crying, my baby nursing, and my husband and I praying for forty-five minutes. Finally, the storm passed and the siren shut off.

My February 21—the day I thought everything would turn around—had turned into a nightmare.

We hugged each other tightly as we went to sleep that night, and I prayed in gratitude that nothing had happened. The next day my friends laughed as I told them the story. Turns out there had not been a tornado near our home—only one somewhere else in our huge county. The siren had been broken. It was not meant to wail continuously, but only in short bursts.

My friends thought the story was funny—things tend to happen to me in strange ways—but I knew it had been God. God must be crystal clear when trying to gain my attention. When crazy things happen, I have a spiritual revelation. It keeps the excitement alive in our relationship. God is the one I should look forward to, not a date.

Of course, I knew this fact, but putting it into practice is usually a different story. Later, as I was rocking my son to sleep in the nursery, I thought back to when I was first a Christian, when I eagerly sought God and needed him as my strength and support. Now I once again relied on others to fill the void. I looked to TV, books, and people to bring me joy. My relationship with God had become lukewarm. I still loved God and sometimes read his Word. I prayed and still had moments of peace, but my daily life was filled with busyness that often took me away from him. My life was filled with friendships, family, and work, but not with God. I was too busy to notice how far away I had strayed from him. Now that he'd moved me into a new situation, I realized how much I still needed him.

I told God I wanted him back. I wanted my relationship with him to be different. I wanted my love for him to be like it was when I was first a Christian—when everything came alive, when I was excited to see how my day would go and watch the things God would do. I wanted my first love back. I asked him how I could get my relationship back, and he turned my focus to my Bible. I would need to read my Bible from start to finish again. I hadn't done that since I'd left Albania. I'm an avid reader and can read a good fiction book in a day. I love to escape. I love to envision the characters and go to an imaginary world. I decided I would read my Bible nightly instead of novels.

I began reading God's precious words consistently for the first time as an older Christian. I read the stories of my youth through the eyes of someone who had failed as a Christian. Slowly, as the Holy Spirit gave me insight into his Holy Word, I started to change. I began to connect to God again and actively seek him. I wanted to learn and know more. I picked up books by other Christian authors and started reading their insights. I fell in love with God in a different way. I started listening to Christian music, and it helped me to stay focused on God. The music washed over my soul, and I felt God filling up my lonely places. I missed my home and my girlfriends, but met new friends who loved God and brought new insights into my life.

I could have stayed in my quiet, lukewarm relationship and would have been happy, but I would have always felt unfulfilled. I struggled with wanting to open myself up to healing my broken parts. As I drew closer to God, I felt the bonds of my shame and guilt slowly start to give way. I felt God knocking on the door I had firmly shut in my heart. I felt a new heart begin to grow.

Chapter 9

Murderer

You shall not murder.
Exodus 20:13

One day when my older children were at school and my baby was asleep, I sat down to read my Bible. I came upon the Ten Commandments. I don't know about you, but I like to read through the list and see which ones I have and haven't committed and then tell myself I am not as bad as I could be because there are still some I have not committed.

As I read through the list that day, I felt good about myself until I read, "You shall not murder." As I stared at the line I had read millions of times before, my eyes blurred and I froze. It was as if time stood still and I forgot to breathe. I had never connected the dots before. I am a murderer. I knew I had chosen to kill those babies, but had never connected that with the fact that it made me a murderer.

Killing something and murder are different things. You can kill someone or something accidentally, or because you expect the other person to harm you—that's self-defense. Planning out the death of another is murder. I had planned and sought out both of my abortions—they were not accidental or because I was being harmed. I had simply decided that my life was more important than the life growing inside me. I had not planned my pregnancies, but I had planned the death of both my babies.

I could give a million reasons why I chose murder. I could write a book defending my choices. Instead, I choose to identify myself as a murderer—the worst kind—because I murdered an innocent.

Once a baby is born, we would never dream of killing it, but our society seems to disagree about murder while the baby is still inside the womb. Our society does not classify the unborn as human—a real being. Many debates have been waged about when those cells inside a woman's body become a living being. When does life truly begin? Is it at the first heartbeat, the first kick, when fingers and toes are formed, the moment when the baby feels pain inside the womb? Or is it at the first breath outside the womb? When do these cells become worthy of being called a life?

I choose now to believe that life begins when the egg and sperm meet. My evidence? God's own words: "For you created my inmost being; you knit me together in my mother's womb" (Psalm 139:13). I choose to believe that God—our Creator—gives us life as he is forming us in our mother's womb. If God, the Creator of the universe, reaches down and takes time to invest in our lives while we're still in our mother's womb, who am I destroy that life?

I know that many people choose not to believe this fact. Some say each woman has the right to choose if she wants to be pregnant and if she wants to have a baby. The debate becomes about *us rather than* the *life inside us.*

One of humanity's biggest downfalls is our arrogance. We could have been happy and had a perfect life walking with God in the garden, but like our first parents, we don't simply want to walk with God. We want to *be* God.

Ask yourself this: Would you allow someone to cut your child—at any age—in half? Would you allow your baby to be thrown into the trash? Of course, you'd say no. Yet that is what I did. It was my choice, and the law backed me up. I know all the arguments. I lived the arguments. I am not judging anyone who makes this choice, but am simply asking you to make sure you *understand* the choice. The choice is murder.

Repeatedly in Scripture we read about people who followed God but then left him. David, Joseph, Moses, and even Peter ran away from God at some point and suffered the consequences. They all suffered as a result of their sins, but then they came back to God. We make choices—God gives us that right—but when we don't like the consequences, we devise ways to remove those consequences and call them choices instead. However, we can't run from those consequences forever.

In the landmark Roe v. Wade case in 1973, the Supreme Court ruled that abortion in the first trimester was legal. Legislation regarding abortion during the second and third trimesters was left to the states. The concurring opinion of Associate Justice Douglas has been summarized as follows: "The Constitution gives women the freedom to make the decision whether to keep an 'unwanted child,' since going through with childbirth can take away the life that the woman intended on."[2] That had been my reasoning too. I had been afraid that the life of my child would take away my life and pose an undue hardship on me. Therefore, I'd chosen to abort my babies.

However, why aren't we talking about not having sex instead? Why aren't we talking about waiting to have sex until we are ready to face the potential outcome? The only reason I can discern is that we want to have our cake and eat it too. We want to have sex when we want, with whom we want, and not have to worry about having a baby. We want to do pleasurable things, but want to remove any unpleasantness or hardship.

I am here to tell you that in my experience, most women who make this choice know deep down they have taken a life. They may not feel like me—full of regret and shame—but they know the consequence of their choice. They may have felt relief about their decision and even felt it was the right thing to do, but they still know they made a choice to take away life.

Murder. It sounds so harsh. As I contemplated the word in my Bible, I found it hard to breathe. The wall holding my sorrow in and away from the outside world crashed down, and I began to cry. I cried for my babies, for myself, and for all the bad choices I had made. I cried for all the people I had hurt, including my parents. When the last tear fell, I looked up and asked God how he could have loved me knowing these horrible things about me. He did not answer me with harsh judgment, nor did I feel a stony silence. Instead, I felt his Spirit fill me with peace. My heart felt lighter as I thought of other Bible verses:

> [He] works for the good of those who love him.
> (Romans 8:28)

> He will never leave you or forsake you.
> (Deuteronomy 31:6)

> Because God has said, "Never will I leave you; never will I forsake you." (Hebrews 13:5)

Of all the steps I had taken so far on this journey, this was the first step to forgiving myself and to full healing.

I first had to take full responsibility for what I had done. I couldn't just play the victim or the loser anymore. I had to look at myself in the mirror and admit I'd done wrong by making those choices. I was a murderer.

As a result of my choice to murder, I made other bad decisions—one after another. Abusing alcohol and drugs, alienating friends, choosing bad partners, screwing up good jobs—the list goes on and on. Now, once I acknowledged I'd made those bad choices, I didn't want to make any more.

I opened the Bible and looked for examples of people like me. I knew the Bible held many examples of murderers, and I wanted to know what they'd done to change their lives. I found that when these people sought God and his will with all their hearts, he forgave them and offered his saving grace.

I started praying. I prayed that God would help me to seek him, that he would hold me close and fill me, and that he would help me make good choices.

I started serving the church more. I spent time talking to the hopeless and helpless. I taught a class for preteens. Most of all, and aside from my works, I held on to God. I focused on his love, and I served. When I looked at my children, I realized that even though

I'd murdered two of his children, God had entrusted me with more of his precious souls. In my heart, I knew I was a murderer, but I also knew I was loved and forgiven. Now God could use me to help people.

During this time, I met a woman who'd had an abortion prior to becoming a Christian. Although she might have been ashamed and guilt-ridden before coming to Christ, once she became a believer she let the shackles of those feelings fall away. Unabashedly, she began sharing her story and allowing her voice to be heard. She spoke out against abortion and made many church presentations in support of the pro-life movement. She did not judge, but recounted how she'd come to know God's saving grace through her choices. She was both welcomed and condemned. People—church people—judged her and told her she was awful and unworthy. (If we can't get the judgment out of the church, how are people supposed to recover from their sins?)

I wondered how she could be so vocal about a choice she'd made herself, especially when faced with so much condemnation from others. When I spoke to her privately, I realized she understood me and all I'd been through. Perhaps only someone who'd made the same choices could understand what the decision to abort does to your soul. She felt horrified by her decision, but was willing to forgive herself and let God's love heal her. I knew I needed to forgive myself. God forgave me, so why couldn't I forgive myself?

I felt that I needed to punish myself for my choices, in the same way that I felt I ought to feel pain for the pain I'd caused. Along the way, I had let my shame and guilt become a part of who I was—daily beating myself up for my choices. When other bad things happened in my life, I'd say it was because I deserved it. I held on to the familiar guilt and shame because it was comfortable. Forgiving myself meant facing the guilt and shame, the bad decisions. Letting go of that comfortable place—despite the pain and hurt I felt while residing there—frightened me. But now I was a Christian, and God called me to be more. He called me to rely on him, not on the feelings I'd created. How could I show others the saving grace of God—to be light to the world—if I didn't accept it for myself?

I had to lay the guilt and shame down. I could no longer keep them in a memorial in my inner room. I had to break the door down and let the light in. I had to stop letting the darkness of my choices define me. I acknowledged my decisions, my pain, and my sadness. I acknowledged the loss of my babies. I acknowledged that I had acted out of fear and selfishness.

Yet acknowledging my faults and mistakes meant steeling myself for possible condemnation from others. I would have to steer myself past the judgment of others, past the raised eyebrows and shocked looks when I told my story. I'd need to work past the insecurity of what others thought about me. I would need to rely on God as he asked me to, knowing that he had forgiven me and that I had fully accepted his grace. I had to let God use my pain and bad choices to grow me. I had to be willing to be whatever he wanted me to be.

As I walked beside God during this time, I felt his arms carrying me. I acknowledged that my God was greater than these things and knew I was more than my choices in his eyes. Even if I messed up again, he would wait for me with open arms, ready to receive me back at any time. His Word says, "My beloved is mine and I am his" (Song of Solomon 2:16). His love never ends, and he calls me his.

I began to fill my life with God's words, and he filled me with his Spirit. Now as I talked about my abortions, I did not feel shame—only God's peace. I allowed myself to breathe and unbind the hurt inside. I filled the broken space with these words: "The LORD your God is with you, the Mighty Warrior who saves. He will take great delight in you; in his love he will no longer rebuke you, but will rejoice over you with singing" (Zephaniah 3:17).

If he could rejoice over me with singing, I could sing his praises with eyes raised high. If he delighted in me, I could delight in myself. If he wouldn't rebuke me, I would not become a slave to my shame, guilt, and fear. "Show me the wonders of your great love, you who save by your right hand those who take refuge in you from their foes. Keep me as the apple of your eye; hide me in the shadow of your wings" (Psalm 17:7–8).

God saved me by his right hand. He had looked over all the earth and stopped to touch *me*. I can't believe I am the apple of his eye. Not only does he love me, but he *actively* loves. When he looks at me, God sees a part of himself. "Then God said, 'Let us make mankind in our image, in our likeness'" (Genesis 1:26).

There is something in me that is in God. Something in me shares his likeness and image. Doesn't this make you pause? None of us have ever seen God, but we have often felt him. Have you longed for more? Do you hear the cry in your soul to be a part of him who created you? Often we don't listen, but for those who do, fulfillment comes. We are not the center of the universe. We are not God—there is something more. We are part of our Creator, and our inner being wants to connect with him.

Choosing not to forgive myself had formed a wedge between God and me. I decided to let that unforgiveness go. I acknowledged what I did—took responsibility—and grieved for my choices. I cried. I got angry. I accepted it. Then I decided to let it go. It wasn't easy. I still look at my abortions as a time I ruined my life. However, I no longer beat myself up for those choices. I allow myself to feel the grief and then fill myself up with God's words of love for me instead. Sometimes it is hard, but I quickly return to God's Word for refreshment and healing. It is there any time we need it.

I continue to read the Bible daily and let his words wash over me. As I get to know God's ways better, I feel better. I feel hemmed in, but not in a bad way. It is in a protected way: "You hem me in behind and before, and you lay your hand upon me" (Psalm 139:5).

I feel more freedom to make choices in my life. I no longer feel trapped by indecision. I rest in his arms and know his love, and our love can cover over a multitude of sins:

> Above all, love each other deeply, because love covers over a multitude of sins. (1 Peter 4:8)

> There is no fear in love. But perfect love drives out fear, because fear has to do with punishment. The one who fears is not made perfect in love. We love because he first loved us. (1 John 4:18–19)

I can love more freely. I can be the friend that others want. I can judge less and help more. I can be more like God. But only because I choose to let him. I choose to accept him. I choose to allow him to fill up my dark places. I choose to pray and read his Word. I choose him daily. I am by no means perfect—I'm a murderer after all—but his grace makes me perfect. You can stand up under his love, but no one can stand up under judgment. I let God change me. He chose me. He wanted to love me and forgive me. Now I willingly follow and trust him.

Chapter 10

A New Calling

*Trust in the LORD with all your heart and lean not on
your own understanding; in all your ways submit to him,
and he will make your paths straight.*
Proverbs 3:5–6

My path continued straight toward God. Now that I no longer held on to my pain, I was like a captive who had been freed. I wanted to do more for him. I wanted to make my Rescuer proud.

Many times in my life I have prayed prayers I would later regret. This time I knew better, but I still let my emotions of freedom get the best of me. I had read an incredible book, *The Circle Maker* by Mark Batterson, and decided I needed to up my game in my prayer life. So I started praying for many things—everything. My biggest prayer? Asking God to show me my purpose directly through a dream or a vision.

As much as I want God to talk to me or an angel to come down and visit me, I know I would freak out if such a thing happened. If I even saw a ghost, I'm not sure I would recover. The Bible is full of stories about spiritual battles, but I don't want anything evil coming for me either. I had no business asking God to do the supernatural with me. At the time, I didn't think it all through.

I also prayed to get back to my pre-pregnancy weight. I had priorities, but my prayer life still needed work.

Humans are often shortsighted. When we feel discomfort or dissatisfaction in any moment, we simply pray for better times, healing, or success instead of failure. It seems simple. However, when the moment passes, our prayers quickly switch to the next thing we need prayer for. We can only live in the moment—we can't see the road ahead. We cannot predict the future, but God knows. Sometimes he answers our prayers not in the moment, but for the future moment.

Prayers are powerful. Prayer works. God wants to answer us. God wants good things for us. God wants us to seek him. He wants us to want him above all.

Proverbs 3:5–6 speaks about leaning on God. Since the day I had recommitted myself to following Jesus while rocking my son, that is what I have done. I read through four different Bible translations. I walked miles in prayer. I allowed my deepest places to be exposed and faced the ugliest parts of me. I worked on forgiving myself by infusing myself with his Word. Through it all, God guided me.

However, I was no closer to understanding his purpose for me. I prayed every day that his will would be done. I prayed that my time would be his time, and I waited. I waited for him to come to me. I kept busy spreading God's love and serving my family and others. I looked for signs, but in the end, I simply waited.

I hate waiting. I like doing. Action defines my self-worth. If I am doing something big, I think I am doing good. If I am successful, then I am smart. In my early years, I would say yes before even thinking about the consequences. (And look where that got me.) I wanted to keep moving, but it felt like God was asking me to wait.

I wanted others to think I was great too. Do you know how hard it is for a stay-at-home mom who gets her sense of self-worth from doing big things to achieve that self-worth from changing diapers, cleaning the house, making dinner, and doing laundry? There are not a ton of awards or financial benefits from being a stay-at-home mom. However, I chose to stay at home with my kids and wouldn't change it for anything, but it was hard to define my purpose during that time. I needed God to *tell me* my purpose.

I am not necessarily a charismatic Christian—I believe in the Spirit and his works. I know that all the things that happened in the early days of Christianity can happen today. I often wonder why they don't. Perhaps it is an issue of faith. I only knew that God had brought me this far—through the pain of abortions and the abuse of drugs and alcohol—and I knew he could show me my purpose too. I believed he would literally *tell* me or *show* me what it was. I prayed and waited. As with most things we pray for, God often wants us to take many steps before we're ready to hear what he has to say. This time was no different.

One of my close friends in Nashville became my walking partner. We clocked many miles each week as we talked with each other about our individual histories. We talked about music and how it impacted us—especially a particular indie artist we both loved. She was coming to Nashville, and we bought tickets. During the opening act, I realized I hadn't listened to any of this artist's music since college. I remembered how opinionated she could be in her music, and I realized I'd left that opinionated life behind. Revisiting those times felt weird now. I looked at the old and young faces of the people around me and realized I was no longer one of them.

As the opening act left the stage, a video played on the monitors. The content of the recording shocked me. I had no idea that this artist's concerts had morphed into pro-choice events. I watched and listened as many different women and doctors appeared on the screen talking about how important it was to have the choice of abortion. The main speaker talked about how she'd had eight abortions and how she thought abortions were just another form of birth control. Her callous remarks and hardened heart hurt me. I felt frozen as I listened to more medical doctors and pro-choice workers speak about similar experiences. The video seemed to be a rallying cry for women to fight for their freedom of choice, to fight for their right to terminate a pregnancy. I looked at all these activists and supporters and wondered how many had abortions.

Politically, I am not trying to take away a woman's ability to choose abortion. Even if the laws change, people will still have abortions. Many women say, "I support pro-choice but would never have an abortion." I want to ask them why. Why would you let your sister make a choice you think is wrong?

I am personally begging you not to make this choice. I know it's the wrong choice. I'm living proof that this choice stays with you, affects you, and haunts you forever. Choosing abortion will change the direction of your life, but not in the way you might think. Having an abortion is not the easier choice. When we make this choice, we will have to give an accounting for the blood we have spilled.

> And for your lifeblood I will surely demand an accounting. I will demand an accounting from every animal. And from each human being, too, I will demand an accounting for the life of another human being.
> (Genesis 9:5)

I believe I will have to give an accounting for my choices. I believe that Jesus's blood covers my sins, but I will still have to stand before my God knowing what I did and give an accounting.

When the video ended, the main singer took the stage and everyone cheered. Still numb from the callous video, I could not join them. The singer took the microphone and yelled that we were going to keep our rights and our freedoms—that abortion was our choice. Everyone in the audience except me and my friend stood up and cheered. I looked around and saw every woman in the audience cheering for their freedom, and I wondered if they knew the shackles that would bind their souls. I wondered if there was a voice for the people like me who'd had abortions and knew abortion was wrong, knew that choice was life-altering, knew the depths of hatred one could have for oneself, and knew that choice would be with you forever. I wondered if there was a voice for us— someone who could tell others not to go this route.

I knew abortion was wrong, but who was I to judge? I'd never felt I had the right to tell women not to choose abortion because I would be considered a hypocrite. So I'd kept silent. As I looked around that room and heard the cry for "freedom," I realized for the first time that this is a war—a war for the unborn, wrought with death.

At that moment, I told God I would be the voice for women

like me if he wanted me to. I would share my story.

My emotions were running high. I didn't know what my promise meant. I simply wanted to show people the destructive results of abortion. I wanted to help just one sister who regretted her choice and lived with the guilt and shame I had. I wanted to be a voice for people like us.

The concert passed quickly. I felt nostalgic hearing the songs of my college years, but as I look back now, I realize the gravity of that moment. God had brought me to a pro-choice concert while making me listen to songs from my college days that would bring up a multitude of emotions.

I felt a tad off balance as we left the concert. This was the first time I had revisited my past since I'd written in my recovery journal all those years ago. My mind raced with ideas. I decided to write a letter to the artist explaining the heartache and pain that can result from the decision to abort a pregnancy. In a five-page letter, I poured out my heart to her. But I never sent the letter. Fear once again kept me from taking that step. I kept walking in prayer circles and wanting to be a voice, but did not know what to do or how to do it.

Then I decided to write a book. I had never written a book before. I did not even know how many pages it should be, how many words it should have, or where I should start. Yet once I had decided to tell my story, I began to write.

Recalling my past and writing about it proved to be difficult. I had to envision everything I had done and revisit how I had felt. I had to try to understand the why. It took me six months, and I wrote only 9,000 words. However, when I finished the final page that spring, I felt proud of myself. I had set out to write a book, and I had—although it was a rather short one. I had no clue if it was good, and I felt exposed and vulnerable now that my story had been written down. My innermost thoughts and feelings were now displayed in black and white to be judged and commented on by others. I wondered if the people from my past life would be upset or feel condemned or criticized by my words. I didn't know what to do with the manuscript, but I felt like I needed to keep pushing forward. I kept remembering the cries of the women in that concert screaming yes as I said no.

I wanted other people's opinions, so I sent my story to some of my closest friends. Although I did get some positive comments, they offered no real direction about what to do next. Once again, I wanted someone to tell me what to do. For the next year, I would send the story to a friend here and there, but would often not hear back or would hear only a couple words of encouragement. Eventually, my husband's company decided to move us again, so I said goodbye to my friends and closed the door on my book.

Despite our move, the book stayed on my mind. I knew God was prompting me to do something more with my words. I began to feel an urgency to have it ready by the next pro-life march, which is held every January in Washington, DC. However, I still didn't know how to turn my words into a viable book. Months passed as I prayed and waited.

Throughout my thirties, my tribe of women had formed a birth community—inviting each other into our births. Most of us in the group had read *The Red Tent* by Anita Diamant. It spoke of the sisterhood of sharing birth, and we wanted that connection with each other. I remember the first time I watched a baby being born. My heart soared as my friend pushed with all her might. I saw the baby's hair, and we heard the first cry. I know watching childbirth is not for everyone, but for me, allowing someone to experience the amazing moment a child is born is a beautiful thing. I welcomed sharing my births with other women. Eight people attended my first birth, three my second, and ten my last.

During this time I met a young mom who was also a doula, and we became close friends. As we talked, I became more interested in becoming a doula too. I felt the Holy Spirit leading me to do something more. I had investigated becoming a birthing coach over the years, but the training was expensive, and I had been busy with my own babies. Now that my children were older, I looked for a program that dealt with childbirth and death, and I discovered one that was reasonably priced. Two weeks later, I signed up to take the courses.

The class was hard, but exhilarating, and I felt myself sucking up the information. I learned all about conception and the birth cycle and wanted to know more. Things I hadn't really understood during my pregnancies now made sense. For the first time, I felt like I was on track to finding my purpose.

I'd enrolled in a specialty program in which I would also be trained in dealing with fatal infant diagnoses and stillbirths. The literature included countless pictures and stories of women who'd had miscarriages and stillbirths, women who had decided to continue their pregnancy even though they knew their baby would die at birth, and women who chose not to carry on their pregnancies after a fatal diagnosis.

As I looked at the pictures and read the stories, my grief resurfaced. That literature reminded me of those pamphlets I'd been given so many years ago. I stared at one little picture of a twelve-week-old baby, saw all the fingers and toes, and thought about how I'd once classified this as just a bunch of cells. I looked at twin babies who were eighteen weeks old and thought about how our country doesn't even call them babies yet at that stage. They looked perfect to me. I thought about the mothers who shed tears over these dead babies and wondered who shed tears for the countless unwanted dead babies. My own tears began to fall, and again a dam broke within me. Going through this course reminded me once again what I had done.

This time, however, instead of letting the self-doubt and judgment take hold, I found refuge in the One who created me. This course became another wave of healing prompted by my God: "He will cover you with his feathers, and under his wings you will find refuge; his faithfulness will be your shield and rampart" (Psalm 91:4). I love that verse and held on to these words as I did my classwork and finished my course.

One of the course requirements was to write a book report on two books from the selected reading list. I chose to read a book about abortion. I didn't know when I chose the book that it was an account of a woman who had been an abortion doctor. I am not sure if I would have chosen that book had I known. She wrote about a girl whose dad had impregnated her, a girl who had been raped, women who simply weren't ready to become mothers, and young girls forced to terminate their babies by their parents. I cringed at these sad and horrible tales. I thought about these women and wondered where they were now.

After I'd read the book, I acknowledged this author's journey. Her heart had only been to help people. She had chosen to give up time with her own family to help women terminate their pregnancies. She thought she was helping, but even she had her limit. She refused to perform abortions for clients who were more than fourteen weeks along in their pregnancy. This was not a law, but her choice. I wondered why.

Again the questions came to mind. When is a baby a baby, and when is ending a pregnancy murdering a child? Everyone needs to ask these questions and figure out the answer. Don't put it out of your mind or support pro-choice views without first considering these questions. It is not about choice; it is about what is right. We can make any choice we want, but there are consequences. I can murder someone today. Maybe I will go to jail or maybe I won't, but I can still make that choice.

Reading *The Common Secret* by Susan Wicklund helped me to see the human side to her decision to perform abortions. She also wrote about how vigilantes would gun down abortion doctors. Those people weren't right either. Two deaths don't make a right. Her story helped me to see how approaching this issue with courage, grace, and empathy is the only way to help people. I now could understand some of the decisions made by doctors and nurses, and this book reminded me of the kindness I'd received from each. However, just because people are kind does not mean they are doing what is right.

In her book, the doctor mentioned that women often walk away from an abortion feeling happy, elated to be free of the burden of motherhood. However, she failed to mention the aftereffects. I knew the truth about how it felt *after* I'd left those clinics. My true feelings had haunted me for years.

I thought about how I had felt giving birth to my first daughter. Before my due date, my friends talked about their birth stories and what would happen during childbirth. I read book after book on what to expect. I felt prepared. Not until after she was born, though, did I realize that the pain of birth doesn't end when the baby is born. No one told me about the bathroom problems I would have, the battle scars I would endure from the endless pushing, or the stitches left behind. I wasn't prepared for the pain of my uterus growing smaller or the inconvenience of the bleeding. The emotional highs and lows—the hormones that would make me feel on top of the world one moment and in the deepest pit the next—affected not only me, but those around me as well. It constantly seemed as if failure was right around the corner. I feared that I would somehow ruin my daughter. No one talked about these things. Abortion comes with many aftereffects, too, and no one talks about them either. That's why I'm talking about them now.

I know some women can make this choice and never think about it again. I know some women feel abortion is simply a means of birth control and choose to abort many times. But I also know there are women out there like me—fearful young women who didn't know what to do and who made a choice that brought them shame and guilt instead of the freedom they were promised.

I'm here to say, even if you've learned to live with your choice, I see you. I acknowledge you and your hurt, shame, and guilt. I know what this choice is like, and you will be okay. Our God is big enough. Even if you don't believe in him, you can take a step toward real freedom. You can forgive yourself. You can let go. But first you must face the choice you made. You are not alone. There are other hurting souls out here with you.

After twelve weeks, I received my doula certificate, specializing in birth and stillbirth. It had been hard work, but I'd done it. I felt a sense of accomplishment, which made me feel like I could do more. I wanted to start helping women navigate the birthing process as well as the process of having to say goodbye to their babies. The timing, however, felt off. We had just moved to a new state, and I did not yet have reliable babysitters. I knew that a woman's labor and delivery didn't follow a firm timeline. My husband's and the kids' schedules would make it difficult to put my doula responsibilities first. So I kept praying for God to tell me what he wanted me to do. I knew I had a purpose, but resigned myself to that purpose being fulfilled in the little things in life while dreaming of bigger things.

As a child, my mind was always lost in the clouds. I never wanted to do anything small. I wanted to be the first female fighter pilot in the Air Force, the first female president, or the next Julia Roberts. I wanted to live life to the fullest and never look back.

As I've aged, some of those dreams have been shelved or discarded because I realized they centered around me. I had wanted the praise and glory. I realized I still wanted the praise, even though I was saying all the right things about giving God the glory. When God began to crack my brokenness and fill it with his love, I realized the glory is for God alone. The first thirty-some years of my life had been about me seeking glory, making choices for myself, and trying to fix things but failing miserably. Now I knew that every good part of me was a gift from God, and I needed to give him the praise.

I began serving him without taking any credit. I relished taking care of the lost and broken—handing a homeless person money or food, seeing their eyes light up but walking away before they could thank me. I focused on giving God the glory for those moments, but I still wanted to do more. I wanted to give more to the God who brought me out of the depths of despair. I continued to pray every day that his will would be done and that he would use me to fulfill his purposes. God began to fill me more and more with his love and purpose.

In March, one of my best friends came to visit me with her son. She had been a faithful friend since my early days as a Christian. The comfort we shared in our friendship comes only from having a long history together. I showed her all the sights of my new town, and as we laughed and talked, I shared with her about the book I had written. Because she is a straightforward person, I knew I could trust her to be honest with me about it. She agreed to read the book, and I emailed it to her.

About a month later, she responded. Her first impression? That at only nine thousand words, it was too short to be called a book. Then we talked about its purpose: Why had I written it? Who was I trying to reach? She advised me to make my message clearer. As she asked her questions, the ideas began to percolate. An endless list of possibilities ran through my mind as we talked, but the choices seemed overwhelming. Should I shorten my book to make it more suitable for pro-life centers? Should I make it a workbook? Although my friend's input spurred many ideas, I still didn't know where to begin. We talked off and on about my book until summer break when my three kids were home every day. As I started to get busy with all the summer activities with them, I became more excited about the possibilities of my book but had no time to work on it.

One morning in late June, God finally answered my prayer. In a dream, I talked with God. He asked who would help him fight the battle to save the lives of his children. Of course, I said, "I will." Then he asked me why I was waiting. He reminded me that countless babies were dying every day. "Okay, I will do it," I said. "I will write the book. I will be your warrior for the lost babies." I woke up with a new purpose burning in my heart.

That morning I knew what he wanted me to do. I knew I had to write this book and that I must accomplish it quickly. Every day that passed, more souls were lost to this earth. I was convinced this was his plan for me. It was confirmed by how quickly God gave me the words.

My nine-thousand-word version had taken over six months to write. As I began my new book, I wrote nine thousand words in the first four days. Within two months, I had written over forty-three thousand words. I'm not a writer. I did not take writing courses in school. In fact, my older brother used to write my essays. I'm a horrible speller. I should not have been able to write all those words so quickly. Yet I did, and that's how I know this was God's purpose for me and a way to bring him all the glory.

My glory-seeking heart would never have written this book. This book details every bad thing I have ever done. However, it also points out every glorious thing my God has accomplished despite my bad choices. God asked me to write this, and as I have obeyed, I have healed even more. I have poured myself into this book, opening all the dark corners and hidden rooms in my heart and laying them bare. In my writing, my brokenness came to light, showing me how that one choice affected me forever. Although I no longer hate myself, I still have scars. I still second-guess my decisions. Sadness still overcomes me when I envision the little ones I aborted. I still wonder what my life would have been like if I had chosen life for my babies. With death there is no chance to live on this earth. Life is so much more hopeful than death. Life speaks of promise. Life speaks of love.

I can look back on my journey and see how everything led to writing this book. I see how God's gentle guidance brought me to this place. Some days I still waver. Is this really what he wants? What are the next steps? Was all this time spent writing wasted? Writing a book is no easy feat, and I pray my words will not be wasted.

I don't know what God's plan is for this book, but I'm being faithful to him in writing it. If this book helps even one girl say no to abortion, it is worth it. If this book helps one broken soul find peace, it is enough.

Many people and organizations have taken up the battle for the unborn. Others have done much more than I will ever do. However, I told God I would be a voice for his truth. I promised him I would share my story so that readers would have insight into the aftereffects of abortion. Those considering abortion should know that their one choice has lasting consequences—not just for the woman, but for everyone affected by that decision.

I share my story for the numerous women I have talked to who feel shame and guilt about their choice. I acknowledge and empathize with them. I understand. I have felt the same shame, guilt, and judgment. However, there is a path toward healing and redemption. It's this path I share with these women—with you. This is my calling.

Every human needs redemption, whether they acknowledge it or not. Redemption comes only through the Father: "In him we have redemption through his blood, the forgiveness of sins, in accordance with the riches of God's grace" (Ephesians 1:7).

We must first acknowledge our need. Next, we face what we've done and allow ourselves to grieve. Finally, lifelong healing comes when we immerse ourselves in the blessed words of our God so that when the Evil One torments us, we have the words to fight. Take his hand and find healing. Redemption is for you.

Chapter 11

The Living, Active Word of God

*For the word of God is alive and active. Sharper than any
double-edged sword, it penetrates even to dividing soul
and spirit, joints and marrow; it judges the thoughts and
attitudes of the heart.*
Hebrews 4:12

The following Bible verses spoke to me when I needed them,
and they continue to speak to me today. Hebrews 4:12 talks
about God's Word being alive and active. This is true in my walk
with God. As I read more of his Word, my heart opens to more of
his will. His Word allows me to see what I have done, but also that
he is willing to forgive. His Scriptures refresh my spirit and bring
me joy daily. I hope the following verses can bring that to your life
as well.

LIFE

Then God said, "Let us make mankind in our image, in our likeness, so that they may rule over the fish in the sea and the birds in the sky, over the livestock and all the wild animals, and over all the creatures that move along the ground."
Genesis 1:26

God created us. Then he trusted us and gave us power to rule over everything he created. He trusted us even though every inclination of our hearts is evil (see Genesis 6:5). We did not have to prove our worth to be trusted or to complete our tasks. It is simply how God created us. He also created us in his image. The word *image* describes how God created us. The next time this word is used in the Bible is when Adam uses it to describe his son. Think about this. God is saying we are a part of him just like our children are a part of us. When he created us, he gave us the power to rule and the ability to choose. He created us in his image. When we choose abortion, we use our power to destroy what was created in his image.

1. Describe how knowing God created us in his image and gave us power to rule makes you feel.
2. Do you believe you are created in his image?
3. If you have chosen to have an abortion, do you believe your choice was to destroy?
4. If you are thinking about having an abortion, describe why you're considering this choice.
5. You have the power to choose—it is God-given. Do you understand, however, that you would be destroying a human made in the image of God? Describe how this statement makes you feel. Do you agree or disagree?

*Then the L*ORD* God formed a man from the dust of the
ground and breathed into his nostrils the breath of life,
and the man became a living being.*
Genesis 2:7

This Scripture looks at the intimacy that God shows us. In every other act of creation, God spoke, and it came to be. I am not sure how close God was to the creation when he spoke. The Bible says he "created" it. However, notice that this Scripture says he "formed" man and breathed into his nostrils, giving him the breath of life. This implies he was close. When God created a woman, he took a part of the man and formed her (Genesis 2:21–22). This again implies closeness. We were brought forth from the womb of Eve. She was the mother of us all.

1. Describe how it feels to know God didn't simply *create* you, but he *formed* you.
2. How do you feel knowing that the breath of life was given to you?
3. Understanding that God breathes life into every human being, do you believe that every life is important, even a person who has done horrible evil?
4. What if Eve had decided not to carry her offspring? Where would that leave us?

*For you created my inmost being; you knit me together in
my mother's womb.*
Psalm 139:13

Each of us called our mother's womb home at one point. We all started there. Before the invention of technology, specifically ultrasounds, people did not know much about the different pregnancy stages. In my mother's generation, they did not do ultrasounds. It was only in the last forty years that technology has allowed us to see the formation of babies in the womb. With this wisdom comes responsibility. We can no longer claim ignorance of life inside the womb. Understand that your life is given to you by the Creator. Realizing that God knit each of us together is key to understanding how valuable life is inside and outside the womb.

1. Describe how it makes you feel to know that God created you by knitting you together in your mother's womb.
2. Describe how it makes you feel that he also knit your baby together in your womb.
3. Would having an ultrasound of your baby affect your decision to abort or keep the baby?
4. After reading this Scripture, when do you think life begins?
5. Do you think we should have the power to take away life?

Before I formed you in the womb I knew you, before you were born I set you apart; I appointed you as a prophet to the nations.
Jeremiah 1:5

This Scripture reminds me that I am not simply my mother or father's child, but I am God's child. God spoke these words to Jeremiah, but they can also be applied to you and the unborn baby in your womb. God has a purpose for every soul he creates. Whether we choose to follow that purpose is up to us. This Scripture makes me wonder what the purpose of my two babies would have been and how they would have affected the world. Knowing God as a living, breathing human being is an incredible experience. Knowing him before we were formed in the womb is unimaginable. We may make many assumptions of what heaven is like and where babies come from, but we really do not know. This Scripture shows us that God knew us before he formed us and has a purpose for each life. Who are we to destroy that?

1. Describe how it makes you feel to know that your baby had a purpose that he or she will no longer be able to accomplish.
2. Describe how it makes you feel to understand that God knew you and your baby before either of you were in the womb.
3. Do you believe that God has a purpose for your life? For your baby's life?
4. If yes, describe how you feel knowing that God has a purpose for your life even now.

~

As you do not know the path of the wind, or how the body
is formed in a mother's womb, so you cannot understand
the work of God, the Maker of all things.
Ecclesiastes 11:5

This Scripture humbles me. It makes me realize that almost nothing is under my control. Although God did give us certain things to rule, many things are out of our control regardless if we believe them or not. Growing old is an exercise in understanding how very little you know and control. We are God's work—his creation. We cannot fully understand the craftsmanship. We cannot fully understand how everything works together; as one mystery is solved, another awaits.

1. Describe how it makes you feel to know that you are in control of very little in this life.
2. Describe how it makes you feel to know that God's ways are different from our ways—his thinking is different from ours.
3. Do you feel like God would condemn or condone abortion?
4. Does this change your thoughts about it?

GRACE

He does not treat us as our sins deserve or repay us
according to our iniquities. For as high as the heavens
are above the earth, so great is his love for those who
fear him; as far as the east is from the west, so far has he
removed our transgressions from us.
Psalm 103:10–12

If, like me, you have had an abortion, there may be a time when you wonder if you could really be forgiven. You may feel like you must treat yourself a certain way because of your decision. You may believe you are not allowed to grieve for your babies, that you shouldn't talk about your choice. You may feel like you will be met with judgment and condemnation. This Scripture showcases how our Father feels about your choice. His love for his children is far-reaching. Like the storybook that says, "I love you to the moon and back," this Scripture reminds us that God's love is as far as the east is to the west and back. He has removed your sin and sees you in a different light. You are forgiven.

1. Describe how it makes you feel to know that God sees you without your sin.
2. Do you understand the extent of God's love for you that it is as far as the east is from the west? Describe what that means to you.
3. Are you able to forgive yourself knowing you are forgiven?

Then I acknowledged my sin to you and did not cover up
my iniquity.
I said, "I will confess my transgressions to the LORD."
And you forgave the guilt of my sin.
Psalm 32:5

Whoever conceals their sins does not prosper, but the one
who confesses and renounces them finds mercy.
Proverbs 28:13

Recognizing your sin and confessing it is the first step in mov-ing toward forgiveness. Talking with God about how you felt, why you made the choice you did, and how sorry you are will bring healing to you. Talking with others and finding a support group can also bring healing. I have talked with many women who told me I was the first person they'd told about their abortion. This is one of the reasons I wrote this book. I want women to open up and no longer hide in shame. In hiding, we allow the Evil One to torment us. If we acknowledge our sin, we will open our heart and soul for healing.

1. In the space provided here, write down how you acknowl-edge your sin to God.

2. Now that you've acknowledged the sin, what can you do to overcome the shame?
3. Describe how it feels to know that God is willing to forgive the guilt you have from hurting another.
4. To get over the shame, we must do the work. Are you willing to do the work? In what way?

Come near to God and he will come near to you.
Wash your hands, you sinners, and purify your hearts,
you double-minded.
James 4:8

He reveals deep and hidden things;
he knows what lies in darkness,
and light dwells with him.
Daniel 2:22

These Scriptures recall the power and love of our Father. He promises that as we come near to him, he will come near to us. Think about that for a moment. The Creator of the universe promises to come near to us, to reveal hidden things, to help us heal. As you go on this journey toward redemption, know that every step you take toward him is being matched by his step toward you. Nothing is in vain.

The second Scripture describes what he has done on my journey. When I first became a Christian, he showed me a little about myself, but as I journeyed toward him, he has revealed more and more. I am at a deeper level of healing because of his revelations. Knowing that light dwells only in him can give us peace and allow us to put our faith in him.

We must choose to come near him. We also must be willing to wash our hands and purify our hearts.

1. What steps do you need to take to wash your hands of guilt?
2. Describe how it makes you feel to know that God is willing to come near you once you've done your part.
3. What steps can you take today to come even closer to God?
4. Take time today to pray that God will reveal your deep and hidden thoughts and emotions about abortion. Pray that his light will dwell deeper in you so that you can rid yourself of the darkness.

I have swept away your offenses like a cloud,
your sins like the morning mist.
Return to me, for I have redeemed you.
Isaiah 44:22

As you work through your shame and guilt, know that if you are a Christian, God has already swept away your sin and offenses. He no longer sees you as a murderer. He sees you as he sees his son, Jesus. His desire is for us to return to him, to turn to him for healing. His heart is to forgive us. He wants us to choose him. He wants to redeem us. If you haven't made a choice to be his, he is waiting for you. He wants to forgive you. He has left that choice up to you. This is another choice that you get to make. This choice, however, leads to eternal life—not death.

1. Do you understand that God gives you a choice to receive forgiveness and have a relationship with him?
2. What is stopping you from choosing his forgiveness and grace?
3. Does shame stop you from receiving forgiveness from God? From yourself? Describe why.
4. Even as a Christian, I have strayed many times and have had to make a conscious decision to return to God. What choices do you need to make to return to God?
5. As you read these Scriptures, do you see that God's grace can cover any sin? Do you understand that there is not one sin he will hold over you if you are redeemed by him? Describe how this makes you feel and what things you will do differently as a result.

LOVE

The LORD your God is with you,
the Mighty Warrior who saves.
He will take great delight in you;
in his love he will no longer rebuke you,
but will rejoice over you with singing.
Zephaniah 3:17

When you have faced the demon of shame, it is hard to lift your head. This Scripture shows us the power of God's love. He doesn't only forgive us, but he also lavishes us with his love. He not only loves us, but he is also with us, saves us, takes delight in us, and rejoices over us. This Scripture will build your faith in how God feels about you so you can, in turn, start to see yourself as the king of the universe sees you.

1. Describe how it makes you feel to know that God is on your side and is willing to save you.
2. What thoughts come to mind when God says he will rejoice over you with singing?
3. If God is willing to take delight in you and no longer rebuke you, are you ready to move toward healing?
4. Do you believe that you deserve healing and forgiveness for your abortion?

~

But when the kindness and love of God our Savior appeared, he saved us, not because of righteous things we had done, but because of his mercy. He saved us through the washing of rebirth and renewal by the Holy Spirit, whom he poured out on us generously through Jesus Christ our Savior, so that, having been justified by his grace, we might become heirs having the hope of eternal life.
Titus 3:4–7

This Scripture brings so much hope to me. It assures me I can never do enough or be enough to earn his grace. God extends his mercy to us out of sheer love and kindness. We are blessed through Jesus and the Holy Spirit. When I read this Scripture, I marvel at God's love for me. He overlooks the murder of one of his children because he loves me. If someone murdered one of my children, I couldn't say that. I wouldn't want to spend eternity with them. However, God's ways are higher than ours, and one day he will wipe away every tear. We will become heirs with the hope of eternal life because his love is greater than anything we choose on this earth. Remember this promise as you work through forgiving yourself.

1. Do you believe you deserve kindness from God? Why or why not?
2. God—who knows many more things than you do—forgives you. Can you forgive yourself?
3. How does it make you feel that we have become heirs to the hope of eternal life?

And hope does not put us to shame, because God's love has been poured out into our hearts through the Holy Spirit, who has been given to us.
Romans 5:5

Shame is one of the worst binders of our spirit. Shame takes root and crushes our ability to move forward, make decisions, go after our purposes, and be happy. Shame is a self-focus that cripples our spiritual life. However, if we focus on God's love and mercy, if we move toward God in our daily life, shame will not be able to take root. Placing our hope in God's love and mercy for eternity will not put us to shame. Our choices may have put us to shame, but God's love never will. He pours out his love for us through the Holy Spirit. The Holy Spirit's purpose is to draw us nearer to God, to help us understand what we need to change, and to know how to walk in God's presence. With the Holy Spirit as our guide and counselor, we can block out the feelings of shame and guilt and no longer be afraid of condemnation. God's love changes, heals, and redirects us to put our hope in the Creator, who loved us enough to save us. God has a plan that will lead you to eternal life. You are free to walk in it.

1. Do you have hope in God's plan? Why or why not?
2. How does it make you feel to know that the Holy Spirit is a gift of God who demonstrates his love for us?
3. Are you willing to let go of your shame and guilt so that God's love can fill in those broken places?

*I pray that out of his glorious riches he may strengthen you
with power through his Spirit in your inner being,
so that Christ may dwell in your hearts through faith.
And I pray that you, being rooted and established in
love, may have power, together with all the Lord's holy
people, to grasp how wide and long and high and deep
is the love of Christ, and to know this love that surpasses
knowledge—that you may be filled to the measure of all
the fullness of God.*
Ephesians 3:16–19

I read this Scripture to my church family the day I committed myself to Christ and was baptized. I read this Scripture as a prayer not just over myself, but over each of them. As I conclude my story, I want you to know that this is my prayer for you. I pray that your broken soul can be filled with the fullness of God. I pray that you understand how willing our God is to find us, love us, and fill us. He has a plan for you. I pray you will find his path for your life. As he guides the steps, I pray you will find peace.

1. Describe how this Scripture makes you feel.
2. Spend some time praying to God to give you the ability to grasp his love and grace for you, and then write down what he has placed on your heart.
3. Take time today to allow God to fill you up with his love.

Notes

1. Robert H. Schuller, *Turning Hurts into Halos* (Nashville: Thomas Nelson, 1999), 16.
2. "Summary: Roe v. Wade (1973)," US Conlawpedia, accessed date, http://sites.gsu.edu/us-constipedia/roe-vs-wade-1973/.

Order Information

REDEMPTION PRESS

To order additional copies of this book, please visit
www.redemption-press.com.

Also available on Amazon.com and BarnesandNoble.com.
Or by calling toll-free 1-844-2REDEEM.

CPSIA information can be obtained
at www.ICGtesting.com
Printed in the USA
LVHW051151280620
659166LV00005B/424

9 781683 149217